BRAIN GAMES®

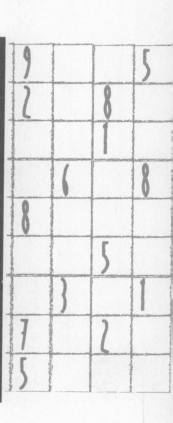

RELAX
AND
SOLVE
SUDOKU

Publications International, Ltd.

Louis Weber, CEO
Publications International, Ltd.
8140 Lehigh Avenue
Morton Grove, IL 60053

ISBN: 978-1-64030-708-7

Manufactured in U.S.A.

8 7 6 5 4 3 2 1

SUDOKU

Use deductive logic to complete the grid so that each row, each column, and each 3 by 3 box contains the numbers 1 through 9 in some order. The solution is unique.

7			2				9	3
9		2	8	7	4			
			5				4	
	9					1	3	2
	6			3			5	
5	2	3					8	
	7				9			
			4	2	8	3		6
3	8				1			5

Answers on page 166.

SUDOKU

Use deductive logic to complete the grid so that each row, each column, and each 3 by 3 box contains the numbers 1 through 9 in some order. The solution is unique.

	5	1		2		9	6	
			8		1			
		2	5		7	1		
	1		2	4	5		8	
5								2
	3		6	1	8		7	
		4	7		2	8		
			4		6			
	7	6		5		2	3	

Answers on page 166.

SUDOKU

Use deductive logic to complete the grid so that each row, each column, and each 3 by 3 box contains the numbers 1 through 9 in some order. The solution is unique.

					5	9	8	
7								
9		5	4	7	3	1		
2		1	3		8	5		
		7	5		1	6		
		9	6		7	3		4
		3	8	1	4	2		6
								3
	4	8	2					

Answers on page 166.

SUDOKU

Use deductive logic to complete the grid so that each row, each column, and each 3 by 3 box contains the numbers 1 through 9 in some order. The solution is unique.

	8		6	9			5	2
1					3			7
			1	2		3		
6		2			1		8	
9		4				5		6
	5		9			2		3
		7		4	6			
3			5					1
5	6			1	9		2	

Answers on page 166.

SUDOKU

Use deductive logic to complete the grid so that each row, each column, and each 3 by 3 box contains the numbers 1 through 9 in some order. The solution is unique.

		9	2	8		7		
		8			7			
2		1				8	4	9
	4			9				3
6			7	4	8			5
8				2			1	
3	8	7				1		2
			8			9		
		4		7	6	3		

Answers on page 166.

SUDOKU

Use deductive logic to complete the grid so that each row, each column, and each 3 by 3 box contains the numbers 1 through 9 in some order. The solution is unique.

					2	3	7	
		8	7	1				5
	3		6					1
	6	9			1			8
	8						2	
3			4			7	6	
4				6			3	
6			8	9	4			
	2	1	3					

Answers on page 166.

LOGIDOKU

The numbers 1 through 9 appear once in every row, column, long diagonal, irregular shape (indicated by marked borders), and 3 by 3 grid. With the numbers already provided, can you complete the puzzle?

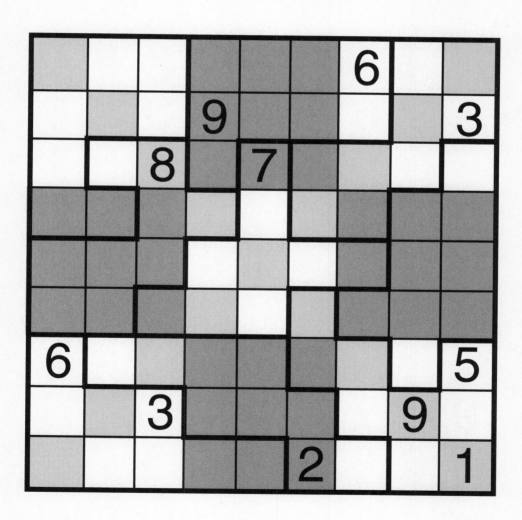

Answers on page 167.

SUDOKU

Use deductive logic to complete the grid so that each row, each column, and each 3 by 3 box contains the numbers 1 through 9 in some order. The solution is unique.

	9	5	3			7	6	
3		6		9		8		1
			1		5			
		3				9		7
	2			1			8	
8		4				2		
			2		6			
9		7		4		1		6
	6	8			1	3	7	

Answers on page 167.

SUDOKU

Use deductive logic to complete the grid so that each row, each column, and each 3 by 3 box contains the numbers 1 through 9 in some order. The solution is unique.

						3		2
	4		2	6		8		
			1			5	6	7
	1	2		4				
	3		8		9		7	
				5		4	1	
5	2	6			8			
		4		2	6		5	
8		3						

Answers on page 167.

SUDOKU

Use deductive logic to complete the grid so that each row, each column, and each 3 by 3 box contains the numbers 1 through 9 in some order. The solution is unique.

4		3	2	9	6			
	2			3	8	6		
	8				5	9		3
2				1	3			
3	4						5	6
			4	5				7
5		2	3				8	
		1	9	8			6	
			5	2	1	3		9

Answers on page 167.

SUDOKU

Use deductive logic to complete the grid so that each row, each column, and each 3 by 3 box contains the numbers 1 through 9 in some order. The solution is unique.

				8		5	6	7
7	4				5			
5		2	3	6		4		
	5		8			1		6
9		8				7		2
2		1			6		8	
		5		4	9	2		3
			1				9	5
6	2	9		5				

Answers on page 167.

SUDOKU

Use deductive logic to complete the grid so that each row, each column, and each 3 by 3 box contains the numbers 1 through 9 in some order. The solution is unique.

6				9	2			4
1	4						9	3
9			4		5	2		
2	6			4	3		5	
			2		9			
	1		6	5			8	2
		6	3		4			5
5	2						3	6
7			5	6				8

Answers on page 167.

SUDOKU

Use deductive logic to complete the grid so that each row, each column, and each 3 by 3 box contains the numbers 1 through 9 in some order. The solution is unique.

9		3				6		1
			2	6	8			
6			1		3			5
	4	8	9		7	3	1	
	6						5	
	9	5	6		1	4	2	
4			8		6			3
			3	1	4			
1		6				7		8

Answers on page 168.

CALCU-DOKU

Use arithmetic and deductive logic to complete the grid so that each row and column contains the numbers 1 through 5 in some order. Numbers in each outlined set of squares combine to produce the number in the top corner using the mathematical sign indicated.

9+	6+	10×		4
		7+	15×	
	2			
5+		2	20×	6×
5	4+			

Answers on page 168.

SUDOKU

Use deductive logic to complete the grid so that each row, each column, and each 3 by 3 box contains the numbers 1 through 9 in some order. The solution is unique.

	4	2	1	6	9			
		1	2					7
							1	9
8				5			7	2
1			3	9	7			4
4	3			2				1
5	6							
3					4	9		
			5	3	8	1	4	

Answers on page 168.

SUDOKU

Use deductive logic to complete the grid so that each row, each column, and each 3 by 3 box contains the numbers 1 through 9 in some order. The solution is unique.

	8		2		4			3
					3	5	4	
		7		5	9	1		
	9	3		2				5	1
	5		7		1		8	
7	1			4		3	6	
		5	3	8		2		
	2	6	4					
8			5		2		1	

Answers on page 168.

SUDOKU

Use deductive logic to complete the grid so that each row, each column, and each 3 by 3 box contains the numbers 1 through 9 in some order. The solution is unique.

7	2		3		6			5
6	4	1						
	5		7	8				
3		7			9			2
		6		3		5		
4			1			6		9
				2	7		5	
						2	7	1
5			9		8		6	4

Answers on page 168.

SUDOKU

Use deductive logic to complete the grid so that each row, each column, and each 3 by 3 box contains the numbers 1 through 9 in some order. The solution is unique.

	4	1						
				3				5
9	3	6	4	8			7	2
8	6		9			7		
1		7	6		8	5		9
		5			1		2	8
7	1			2	9	3	8	6
6				1				
						2	1	

Answers on page 168.

LOGIDOKU

The numbers 1 through 9 appear once in every row, column, long diagonal, 3 by 3 box, and irregular shape. From the numbers given, can you complete the puzzle?

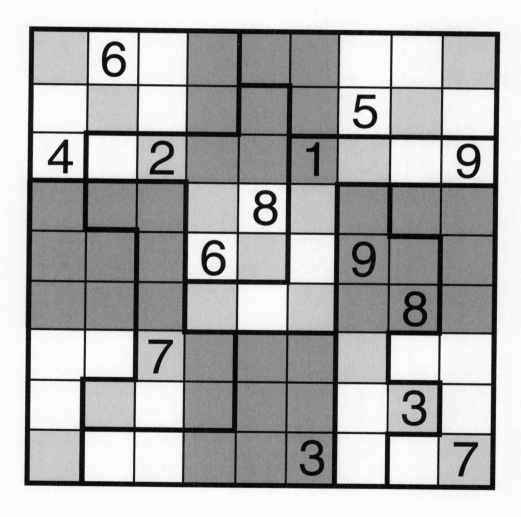

Answers on page 168.

SUDOKU

Use deductive logic to complete the grid so that each row, each column, and each 3 by 3 box contains the numbers 1 through 9 in some order. The solution is unique.

			5	6	7	3	9	
			8	3		6	5	
					9	7	8	2
	5	3						7
7			1		6			8
1					5	2		
9	2	7	6					
	5	1		7	3			
	4	6	2	5	1			

Answers on page 169.

SUDOKU

Use deductive logic to complete the grid so that each row, each column, and each 3 by 3 box contains the numbers 1 through 9 in some order. The solution is unique.

		5	6	9		8	7	
	2		7			9	6	
			8				1	3
	6	9		8	5			1
		4				7		
2			3	1		6	4	
5	7				9			
	8	2			4		3	
	4	6		3	8	2		

Answers on page 169.

SUDOKU

Use deductive logic to complete the grid so that each row, each column, and each 3 by 3 box contains the numbers 1 through 9 in some order. The solution is unique.

9		2				1		6
			1			3		
1			9		2		4	7
	8	6		3		5		
			5		8			
		9		4		2	1	
8	9		3		5			2
		3			6			
4		1				7		5

Answers on page 169.

SUDOKU

Use deductive logic to complete the grid so that each row, each column, and each 3 by 3 box contains the numbers 1 through 9 in some order. The solution is unique.

5		9			8			4
		2	5			1		
	4			9	3		7	8
3		5					1	
		8		7		4		
	9					3		6
2	7		9	6			4	
		6			2	7		
9			8			6		3

Answers on page 169.

SUDOKU

Use deductive logic to complete the grid so that each row, each column, and each 3 by 3 box contains the numbers 1 through 9 in some order. The solution is unique.

	5					2	3	6
	4	3	2		5			7
9		2			6	5		
		1	4	3				9
	9						1	
7				6	1	8		
		9	1			3		5
8			5		4	6	2	
2	1	5					4	

Answers on page 169.

CALCU-DOKU

Use arithmetic and deductive logic to complete the grid so that each row and column contains the numbers 1 through 5 in some order. Numbers in each outlined set of squares combine to produce the number in the top corner using the mathematical sign indicated.

8+	1	7+		7+
	6+		1	
7+		14+	2×	
10+				12×
		3×		

Answers on page 169.

SUDOKU

Use deductive logic to complete the grid so that each row, each column, and each 3 by 3 box contains the numbers 1 through 9 in some order. The solution is unique.

		5	8					
					7	4		6
9	2							
			1	4		8	2	
	7	8		6	3			
							5	8
2		4	6					
					5	1		

Answers on page 170.

SUDOKU

Use deductive logic to complete the grid so that each row, each column, and each 3 by 3 box contains the numbers 1 through 9 in some order. The solution is unique.

	6	4	3	1	8	9	2	
		8		5	6			1
						3		
4			5	2		8		
5	2						1	3
		9		6	3			4
		3						
9			6	3		1		
	8	5	9	7	2	4	3	

Answers on page 170.

SUDOKU

Use deductive logic to complete the grid so that each row, each column, and each 3 by 3 box contains the numbers 1 through 9 in some order. The solution is unique.

	9		5		2		6	
6				1				3
3				2				6
	8		3		1		9	
1				9				7
5				3				8
	2		4		5		7	

Answers on page 170.

SUDOKU

Use deductive logic to complete the grid so that each row, each column, and each 3 by 3 box contains the numbers 1 through 9 in some order. The solution is unique.

6			5					1
	9							
5	4		8					
1		2	7	8			4	
4	7						2	8
	6			2	4	3		9
				3		8	6	
						1		
2				6				4

Answers on page 170.

SUDOKU

Use deductive logic to complete the grid so that each row, each column, and each 3 by 3 box contains the numbers 1 through 9 in some order. The solution is unique.

			2					
5		6			1			2
4		7		6				
2	7						1	
		8				6		
	6						2	7
				3		8		6
1			8			5		4
				5				

Answers on page 170.

SUDOKU

Use deductive logic to complete the grid so that each row, each column, and each 3 by 3 box contains the numbers 1 through 9 in some order. The solution is unique.

2	3	1		5			9	
	4						3	
		8	4					2
	8	6		1		4		
1		9				2		3
		4		7		9	1	
8					2	3		
	1						6	
	9			6		8	2	5

Answers on page 170.

LOGIDOKU

The numbers 1 through 9 appear once in every row, column, long diagonal, irregular shape (indicated by marked borders), and 3 by 3 grid. From the numbers already given, can you complete the puzzle?

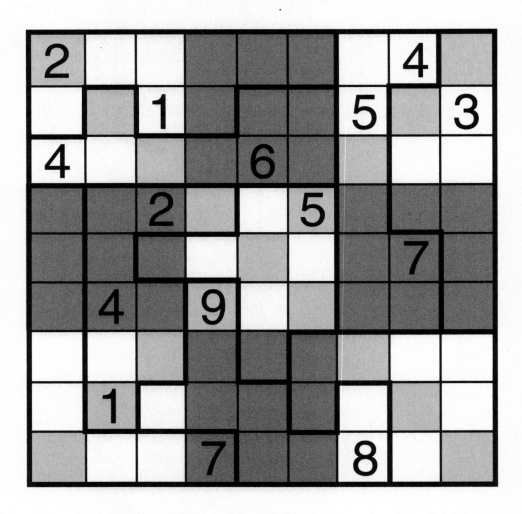

Answers on page 171.

SUDOKU

Use deductive logic to complete the grid so that each row, each column, and each 3 by 3 box contains the numbers 1 through 9 in some order. The solution is unique.

		9		7		2		
1		4				3		9
	3			4			8	
			9		6			
2		8				7		5
			7		8			
	1			8			2	
7		3				5		6
		2		1		4		

Answers on page 171.

SUDOKU

Use deductive logic to complete the grid so that each row, each column, and each 3 by 3 box contains the numbers 1 through 9 in some order. The solution is unique.

				2	7			
		8			1	3		
9				5			1	
2			3	6			5	
	1	9				2	6	
	5			9	2			3
	6			3				5
		3	2			7		
			7	1				

Answers on page 171.

SUDOKU

Use deductive logic to complete the grid so that each row, each column, and each 3 by 3 box contains the numbers 1 through 9 in some order. The solution is unique.

	7						6	
	4			6			3	
6			1		5			9
9		8		4		3		5
				8				
5		2		3		8		1
7			8		4			3
	5			2			1	
	9						8	

Answers on page 171.

SUDOKU

Use deductive logic to complete the grid so that each row, each column, and each 3 by 3 box contains the numbers 1 through 9 in some order. The solution is unique.

5			3			2		
4			6		7	9	5	
6				2	5			
	3							
2				9				7
							8	
			1	6				3
	6	1	7		8			9
		9			2			6

Answers on page 171.

SUDOKU

Use deductive logic to complete the grid so that each row, each column, and each 3 by 3 box contains the numbers 1 through 9 in some order. The solution is unique.

				9	8			
	3	8			7	2	4	
	9						6	
5	4							
6								8
							7	3
	8						2	
	2	6	5			7	3	
			4	6				

Answers on page 171.

CALCU-DOKU

Use arithmetic and deductive logic to complete the grid so that each row and column contains the numbers 1 through 5 in some order. Numbers in each outlined set of squares combine to produce the number in the top corner using the mathematical sign indicated.

6+	7+		30×	
	4−	20×		
9+			3	3+
		8×		
6×			1−	

Answers on page 172.

SUDOKU

Use deductive logic to complete the grid so that each row, each column, and each 3 by 3 box contains the numbers 1 through 9 in some order. The solution is unique.

	6			7		4		
4	8	1	6			3	7	
3			1		4		6	
						2		
	4			6			9	
		9						
	7		5		6			8
	1	4			8	5	3	7
		8		3			1	

Answers on page 172.

SUDOKU

Use deductive logic to complete the grid so that each row, each column, and each 3 by 3 box contains the numbers 1 through 9 in some order. The solution is unique.

			3	6			4	
4		6						
			1	2			9	
						5		9
8		9				1		4
7		3						
	1			9	2			
						4		8
	6			7	8			

Answers on page 172.

SUDOKU

Use deductive logic to complete the grid so that each row, each column, and each 3 by 3 box contains the numbers 1 through 9 in some order. The solution is unique.

3				9			5	
		9		2		8		
	6		4			1		
	3				6		8	9
			2	8	9			
6	9		3			5		
	5				3		1	
	1			7		2		
	4			5				3

Answers on page 172.

SUDOKU

Use deductive logic to complete the grid so that each row, each column, and each 3 by 3 box contains the numbers 1 through 9 in some order. The solution is unique.

	9		3				8	2
	5			2	6	7		
6			9				3	5
	6		7					8
	4					2		
9					8		7	
5	8				7			3
		1	6	5			9	
7	2				1		6	

Answers on page 172.

SUDOKU

Use deductive logic to complete the grid so that each row, each column, and each 3 by 3 box contains the numbers 1 through 9 in some order. The solution is unique.

	1							
3	6			2	8			
		4	5				6	9
1	8				7			
2			8		6			3
			3				8	7
9	5				4	7		
			6	5			9	2
							5	

Answers on page 172.

SUDOKU

Use deductive logic to complete the grid so that each row, each column, and each 3 by 3 box contains the numbers 1 through 9 in some order. The solution is unique.

	4				2			
			8	3	5			4
		8	7			6		
4	1					7	6	
	2			4			8	
	5	9					4	2
		5			8	2		
6			9	2	3			
			6				1	

Answers on page 173.

LOGIDOKU

The numbers 1 through 9 appear once in every row, column, long diagonal, irregular shape (indicated by marked borders), and 3 by 3 grid. From the numbers already given, can you complete the puzzle?

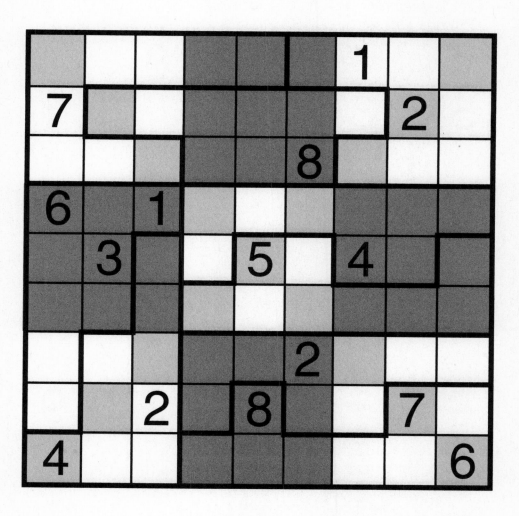

Answers on page 173.

SUDOKU

Use deductive logic to complete the grid so that each row, each column, and each 3 by 3 box contains the numbers 1 through 9 in some order. The solution is unique.

			6		1	8		
5	6	8		7			1	
	1		5	8				
6			1				9	2
		2				4		
8	9				4			6
				9	2		4	
	8			1		7	3	9
		5	7		6			

Answers on page 173.

SUDOKU

Use deductive logic to complete the grid so that each row, each column, and each 3 by 3 box contains the numbers 1 through 9 in some order. The solution is unique.

			4					
	5	2		7				
		3				1	2	
4			7				9	3
		9		8				
8	5			3			6	
	7	8				4		
		5			4	9		
			6					

Answers on page 173.

SUDOKU

Use deductive logic to complete the grid so that each row, each column, and each 3 by 3 box contains the numbers 1 through 9 in some order. The solution is unique.

				2		6	7	3
		4	6	1			5	
			5				4	
3	5				6			4
			1	7	2			
2			5				8	6
	1			9				
	4			3	1	5		
9	8	7		6				

Answers on page 173.

SUDOKU

Use deductive logic to complete the grid so that each row, each column, and each 3 by 3 box contains the numbers 1 through 9 in some order. The solution is unique.

6						8		
1		4			8		7	9
					3			
	5				1			
9		2		4		6		1
			8				3	
			1					
7	8		2			9		6
		5						7

Answers on page 173.

SUDOKU

Use deductive logic to complete the grid so that each row, each column, and each 3 by 3 box contains the numbers 1 through 9 in some order. The solution is unique.

2	3		7	1		5		
					6			
7		4			8	2		
			1					8
8		9		5		7		4
3					4			
		6	3			4		5
			2					
		7		6	5		2	3

Answers on page 174.

CALCU-DOKU

Use arithmetic and deductive logic to complete the grid so that each row and column contains the numbers 1 through 4 in some order. Numbers in each outlined set of squares combine to produce the number in the top corner using the mathematical sign indicated.

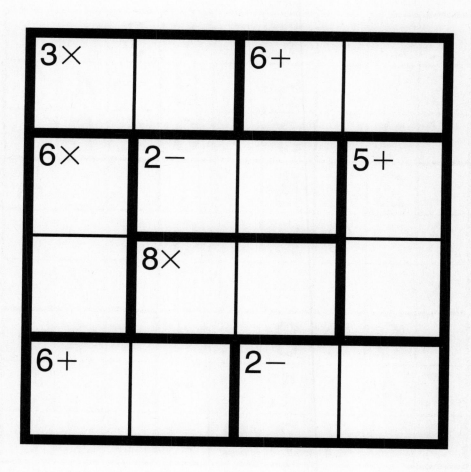

Answers on page 174.

SUDOKU

Use deductive logic to complete the grid so that each row, each column, and each 3 by 3 box contains the numbers 1 through 9 in some order. The solution is unique.

				7	1	9		8
6			5		2		4	3
	9		3		8	1	5	
	2		8					
		9	2		3	6		
					9		7	
	6	2	9		4		1	
7	4		1		6			5
9		3	7	2				

Answers on page 174.

SUDOKU

Use deductive logic to complete the grid so that each row, each column, and each 3 by 3 box contains the numbers 1 through 9 in some order. The solution is unique.

7	2						4	
		8				3		
			9				5	7
		1			4			9
			8	1	3			
5			2			7		
1	6				9			
		5				4		
	9						6	5

Answers on page 174.

SUDOKU

Use deductive logic to complete the grid so that each row, each column, and each 3 by 3 box contains the numbers 1 through 9 in some order. The solution is unique.

2		7			9		4	
	9				2			3
			5					1
6	4					8		
			6		5			
		8					7	6
9					4			
4			8				5	
	7		2			9		4

Answers on page 174.

SUDOKU

Use deductive logic to complete the grid so that each row, each column, and each 3 by 3 box contains the numbers 1 through 9 in some order. The solution is unique.

					8			
				6	5		4	
	8	6	2			5		1
	6		1					2
5								6
4					2		1	
1		3			7	9	6	
	4		3	9				
			8					

Answers on page 174.

SUDOKU

Use deductive logic to complete the grid so that each row, each column, and each 3 by 3 box contains the numbers 1 through 9 in some order. The solution is unique.

8	4			3				
		1		5				
			7				6	9
					8			1
	9	6	5		2	4	8	
5			1					
4	8				7			
				2		7		
				1			3	5

Answers on page 175.

SUDOKU

Use deductive logic to complete the grid so that each row, each column, and each 3 by 3 box contains the numbers 1 through 9 in some order. The solution is unique.

							8	
	9	7		3	6		1	
	8		1			4		3
								5
1			9		5			8
9								
2		1			9		4	
	7		3	5		8	9	
	3							

Answers on page 175.

LOGIDOKU

The numbers 1 through 9 appear once in every row, column, long diagonal, irregular shape (indicated by marked borders), and 3 by 3 grid. From the numbers already given, can you complete the puzzle?

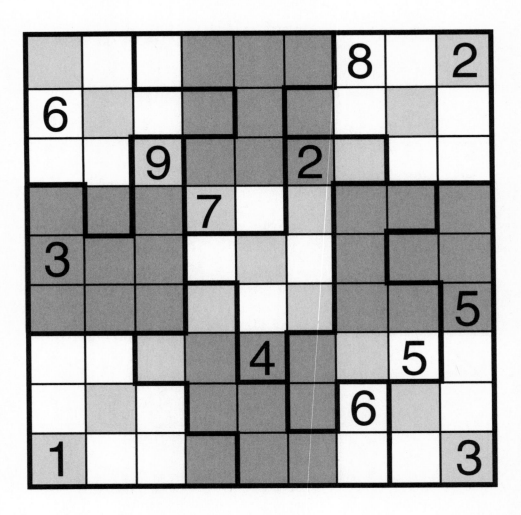

Answers on page 175.

SUDOKU

Use deductive logic to complete the grid so that each row, each column, and each 3 by 3 box contains the numbers 1 through 9 in some order. The solution is unique.

9		2	1	4		5		
	4				6			1
5					2			
	5					1		
	2						4	
		9					3	
			8					3
2			5				7	
		7		2	1	6		8

Answers on page 175.

SUDOKU

Use deductive logic to complete the grid so that each row, each column, and each 3 by 3 box contains the numbers 1 through 9 in some order. The solution is unique.

				3				6
					7	9		
4	8		2			3		
5					3		9	8
				1				
2	9		8					4
		7			4		6	5
		9	6					
1				2				

Answers on page 175.

SUDOKU

Use deductive logic to complete the grid so that each row, each column, and each 3 by 3 box contains the numbers 1 through 9 in some order. The solution is unique.

	7			4			8	
4								2
	1	6	9			3		
		8	2	9				
	6						9	
			8	4	2			
		3			8	1	6	
7								4
	4			5			3	

Answers on page 175.

SUDOKU

Use deductive logic to complete the grid so that each row, each column, and each 3 by 3 box contains the numbers 1 through 9 in some order. The solution is unique.

							8	
8		1			6		5	3
				8	2			
	6		5			7	1	
	5	2				3	6	
	7	9			4		2	
			6	5				
7	1		8			2		5
	3							

Answers on page 176.

SUDOKU

Use deductive logic to complete the grid so that each row, each column, and each 3 by 3 box contains the numbers 1 through 9 in some order. The solution is unique.

			6	9		4		
1		8	5					9
				7		5	6	
4		9	7	2				
			5	6	1			4
	2	1	8					
8				7	2			3
		6		1	3			

Answers on page 176.

SUDOKU

Use deductive logic to complete the grid so that each row, each column, and each 3 by 3 box contains the numbers 1 through 9 in some order. The solution is unique.

		6			8		4	
				6		1		
1	2						6	
7	3	4	5					
	1					3		
				1	4	9	7	
	9						7	1
	2		3					
	5		9		8			

Answers on page 176.

CALCU-DOKU

Use arithmetic and deductive logic to complete the grid so that each row and column contains the numbers 1 through 5 in some order. Numbers in each outlined set of squares combine to produce the number in the top corner using the mathematical sign indicated.

24×		4+		6+
14+		2÷	2÷	
				6×
2−		1−		
1	6×		20×	

Answers on page 176.

SUDOKU

Use deductive logic to complete the grid so that each row, each column, and each 3 by 3 box contains the numbers 1 through 9 in some order. The solution is unique.

9	5			2				
			7				8	
6								
		7		8	6			
					8	2	6	
	7						5	
	3	6	5					
			2	7		9		
	8				3			4
			6				7	1

Answers on page 176.

SUDOKU

Use deductive logic to complete the grid so that each row, each column, and each 3 by 3 box contains the numbers 1 through 9 in some order. The solution is unique.

		8			1			
1		4	9					3
					5		4	
3					6	5		
	2			1			8	
		1	7					9
	1		5					
9					7	2		4
			4			8		

Answers on page 176.

SUDOKU

Use deductive logic to complete the grid so that each row, each column, and each 3 by 3 box contains the numbers 1 through 9 in some order. The solution is unique.

			5		7			
6	3			2				1
	7			6			4	
						8		6
			7	1	6			
4		9						
	2			5			6	
7				8			5	3
			9		3			

Answers on page 177.

SUDOKU

Use deductive logic to complete the grid so that each row, each column, and each 3 by 3 box contains the numbers 1 through 9 in some order. The solution is unique.

2	5				3		6	
		1		4	6		8	
						5		
		5	3	8		6	3	
		5	3		7	9		
	8	3		1				
		2						
	4		2	7		8		
	9		6				4	2

Answers on page 177.

SUDOKU

Use deductive logic to complete the grid so that each row, each column, and each 3 by 3 box contains the numbers 1 through 9 in some order. The solution is unique.

		9	2	6		1		
2			4			3	7	
					9			
	7			8	4			
6								5
		5	2				1	
		1						
	3	7			6			4
		8		7	2	6		

Answers on page 177.

LOGIDOKU

The numbers 1 through 9 appear once in every row, column, long diagonal, irregular shape (indicated by marked borders), and 3 by 3 grid. From the numbers already given, can you complete the puzzle?

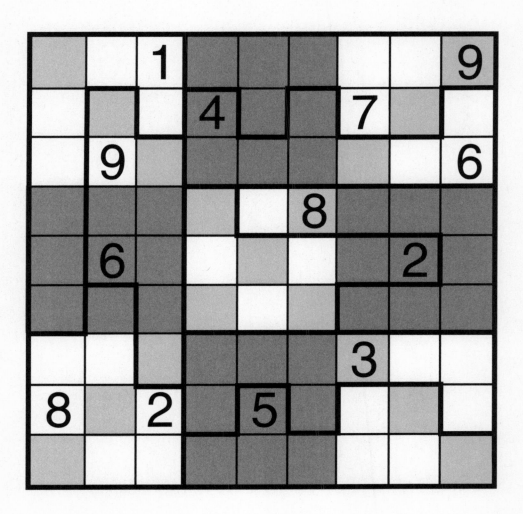

Answers on page 177.

SUDOKU

Use deductive logic to complete the grid so that each row, each column, and each 3 by 3 box contains the numbers 1 through 9 in some order. The solution is unique.

9				2			6	8
1	6						9	
		4			3		5	
					4	9	2	
	4	3	5					
	7		3			6		
	9						1	3
3	1			7				9

Answers on page 177.

SUDOKU

Use deductive logic to complete the grid so that each row, each column, and each 3 by 3 box contains the numbers 1 through 9 in some order. The solution is unique.

	1			6		4	8	
				8			5	1
		9				3		
	6	5			3			
			5		2			
			8			2	9	
		1				7		
4	5			2				
	3	8		9			1	

Answers on page 177.

SUDOKU

Use deductive logic to complete the grid so that each row, each column, and each 3 by 3 box contains the numbers 1 through 9 in some order. The solution is unique.

		6				9		
2								5
		4	7		1	3		
	9		8		7		1	
	7		6		3		9	
		7	5		9	2		
3								1
		1				6		

Answers on page 178.

SUDOKU

Use deductive logic to complete the grid so that each row, each column, and each 3 by 3 box contains the numbers 1 through 9 in some order. The solution is unique.

3			7					5
	9			6			8	
		7	2			3		
						2		7
	1						6	
5		3						
		8			7	6		
	4			5			1	
6					1			9

Answers on page 178.

SUDOKU

Use deductive logic to complete the grid so that each row, each column, and each 3 by 3 box contains the numbers 1 through 9 in some order. The solution is unique.

					8		3	
9	4		5			1		
			7					5
4								1
3		6	4		9	5		8
8								7
5					7			
		2			1		6	4
	3		6					

Answers on page 178.

SUDOKU

Use deductive logic to complete the grid so that each row, each column, and each 3 by 3 box contains the numbers 1 through 9 in some order. The solution is unique.

					3			9
5				6	9	4		
4			8					
			9			5		1
	9			7			6	
7		1			5			
					8			4
		7	1	3				5
2			7					

Answers on page 178.

CALCU-DOKU

Use arithmetic and deductive logic to complete the grid so that each row and column contains the numbers 1 through 6 in some order. Numbers in each outlined set of squares combine to produce the number in the top corner using the mathematical sign indicated.

1−	3+		11+	15×	
	8×			5−	
5−		90×		7+	3+
20×					
3÷	15×		24×		20×
		4+		2	

Answers on page 178.

SUDOKU

Use deductive logic to complete the grid so that each row, each column, and each 3 by 3 box contains the numbers 1 through 9 in some order. The solution is unique.

	7					8		
		6						9
	8		9			1	2	6
				9				4
		8	3	7	5	9		
9				1				
7	9	3			8		5	
2						7		
		4					9	

Answers on page 178.

SUDOKU

Use deductive logic to complete the grid so that each row, each column, and each 3 by 3 box contains the numbers 1 through 9 in some order. The solution is unique.

	4	2					3	
	5			9				
1				8	7			
	6		5					
7	1			4			5	3
					3		7	
			8	5				6
				1			9	
	7					5	8	

Answers on page 179.

SUDOKU

Use deductive logic to complete the grid so that each row, each column, and each 3 by 3 box contains the numbers 1 through 9 in some order. The solution is unique.

	7		2				4	1
					7	9		
2					4		3	
		5	4					8
			8		9			
9					5	6		
	4		9					3
		3	6					
7	9				3		6	

Answers on page 179.

SUDOKU

Use deductive logic to complete the grid so that each row, each column, and each 3 by 3 box contains the numbers 1 through 9 in some order. The solution is unique.

	5						3	9
3		1						
				1		7		
					8	6		1
	9		6	5	4		2	
2		5	3					
		9		8				
						2		4
6	1						8	

Answers on page 179.

SUDOKU

Use deductive logic to complete the grid so that each row, each column, and each 3 by 3 box contains the numbers 1 through 9 in some order. The solution is unique.

				4			9	8
					6			
		9	7				1	6
			8					4
1			9	5	2			3
9					7			
8	7				9	6		
			6					
4	1			3				

Answers on page 179.

ODD-EVEN LOGIDOKU

The numbers 1 through 9 appear once in every row, column, long diagonal, 3 by 3 grid, and irregular shape. Cells marked with the letter E contain even numbers. From the numbers already given, can you complete the puzzle?

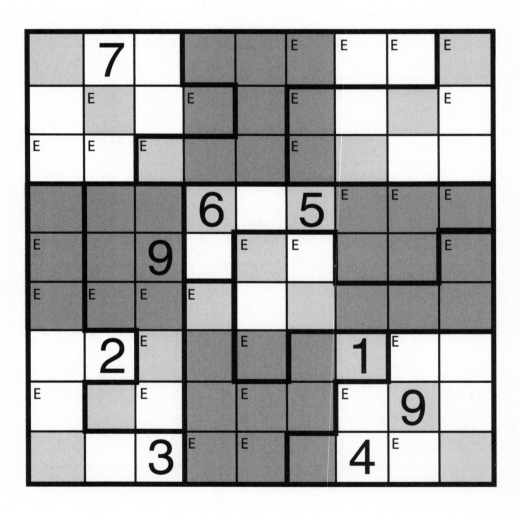

Answers on page 179.

SUDOKU

Use deductive logic to complete the grid so that each row, each column, and each 3 by 3 box contains the numbers 1 through 9 in some order. The solution is unique.

								1
	9	7			3			
			9		6		4	
		9					1	5
6	1						8	9
5	8					2		
	6		8		1			
			7			4	5	
4								

Answers on page 179.

SUDOKU

Use deductive logic to complete the grid so that each row, each column, and each 3 by 3 box contains the numbers 1 through 9 in some order. The solution is unique.

1	6							5
						4		
			4	3			8	
		1	5		3	9		4
				4				
8		7	1		2	3		
	5			1	8			
		2						
3							2	8

Answers on page 180.

SUDOKU

Use deductive logic to complete the grid so that each row, each column, and each 3 by 3 box contains the numbers 1 through 9 in some order. The solution is unique.

					7	3		9
	1		4					7
5		7						
		5		3				
3	7			1			2	6
				6		5		
						8		3
4					3		6	
6		8	1					

Answers on page 180.

SUDOKU

Use deductive logic to complete the grid so that each row, each column, and each 3 by 3 box contains the numbers 1 through 9 in some order. The solution is unique.

	8	4				9		7
1				3	2	6		
			1	4				8
	4		5		8		6	
2				7	6			
		3	4	8				5
8		7				4	9	

Answers on page 180.

SUDOKU

Use deductive logic to complete the grid so that each row, each column, and each 3 by 3 box contains the numbers 1 through 9 in some order. The solution is unique.

			9	1				
		6						7
3		7	4					2
		1	7					8
	4			9			6	
8					2	1		
1					9	8		3
4						2		
				5	1			

Answers on page 180.

CALCU-DOKU

Use arithmetic and deductive logic to complete the grid so that each row and column contains the numbers 1 through 4 in some order. Numbers in each outlined set of squares combine to produce the number in the top corner using the mathematical sign indicated.

10+		16×	
2÷			
	3+	7+	3×
4			

Answers on page 180.

SUDOKU

Use deductive logic to complete the grid so that each row, each column, and each 3 by 3 box contains the numbers 1 through 9 in some order. The solution is unique.

			7					
6		2				1	9	
		8		4	6	2		
						3	8	
8			2		3			9
	6	9						
		3	5	8		6		
	7	5					8	2
					4			

Answers on page 180.

SUDOKU

Use deductive logic to complete the grid so that each row, each column, and each 3 by 3 box contains the numbers 1 through 9 in some order. The solution is unique.

	7				8			
9	5				7	2	1	
		1						
							3	9
	1	9		7		4	2	
5	6							
						6		
	4	3	2				9	7
			3				4	

Answers on page 181.

SUDOKU

Use deductive logic to complete the grid so that each row, each column, and each 3 by 3 box contains the numbers 1 through 9 in some order. The solution is unique.

				1		9		
			7	9	8			
		5						3
	3			8			2	
7	2						9	6
	9			3			4	
8						5		
			5	4	9			
		1		6				

Answers on page 181.

SUDOKU

Use deductive logic to complete the grid so that each row, each column, and each 3 by 3 box contains the numbers 1 through 9 in some order. The solution is unique.

						9	5	
9				5		4	2	3
3			9		2	6		
	2		5	9			6	
	1			6	8		7	
	6	7		9				1
2	9	1		4				6
	3	7						

Answers on page 181.

SUDOKU

Use deductive logic to complete the grid so that each row, each column, and each 3 by 3 box contains the numbers 1 through 9 in some order. The solution is unique.

	1				5			
5	2	4			7			
9			6		8			
6			2	1				
	7						1	
				3	4			9
			4		1			6
			9			8	5	3
			5				7	

Answers on page 181.

SUDOKU

Use deductive logic to complete the grid so that each row, each column, and each 3 by 3 box contains the numbers 1 through 9 in some order. The solution is unique.

					2			4
	7	1			5		3	
4						6		7
		9	2					8
			7		3			
6					4	2		
9		4						6
	2		3			4	1	
7			4					

Answers on page 181.

ODD-EVEN LOGIDOKU

The numbers 1 through 9 are to appear once in every row, column, long diagonal, 3 by 3 box, and irregular shape. Cells marked with the letter E contain even numbers. From the numbers given, can you complete the puzzle?

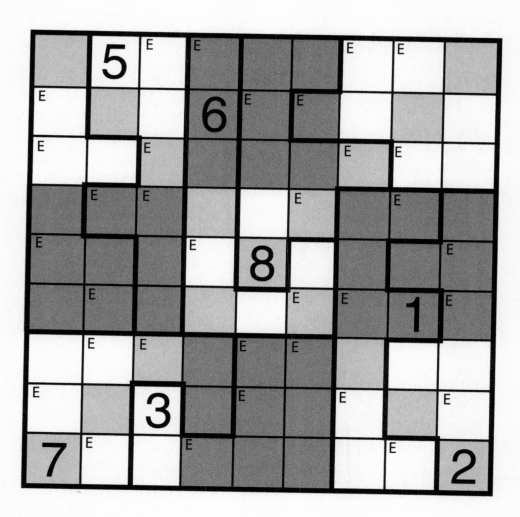

Answers on page 181.

SUDOKU

Use deductive logic to complete the grid so that each row, each column, and each 3 by 3 box contains the numbers 1 through 9 in some order. The solution is unique.

					3			2
		4		6		5		
6	8	1						
	2			5				9
			6		2			
4				9			3	
						6	5	8
		2		4		3		
3			7					

Answers on page 182.

SUDOKU

Use deductive logic to complete the grid so that each row, each column, and each 3 by 3 box contains the numbers 1 through 9 in some order. The solution is unique.

	3			9				
	6	2	4		7			
4	8				6			
1		6						9
		8				3		
3						4		1
			1				3	2
			6		5	8	1	
				4			5	

Answers on page 182.

SUDOKU

Use deductive logic to complete the grid so that each row, each column, and each 3 by 3 box contains the numbers 1 through 9 in some order. The solution is unique.

						3		4
	8							
7		1	9			8	6	
8		3			4			5
				6				
9			8			1		3
	2	5			7	9		1
							7	
3		4						

Answers on page 182.

SUDOKU

Use deductive logic to complete the grid so that each row, each column, and each 3 by 3 box contains the numbers 1 through 9 in some order. The solution is unique.

					7	3		4	
2				5			6		
	7	5							2
7					8			5	
			9						
	8		7						4
5						3	9		
		2			1				8
	6		3	4					

Answers on page 182.

SUDOKU

Use deductive logic to complete the grid so that each row, each column, and each 3 by 3 box contains the numbers 1 through 9 in some order. The solution is unique.

7							3	4
			6	3		5		
		8	5		1			
2		3						7
				6				
4						6		8
		9	7		4	2		
		4		1	2			
8	7							1

Answers on page 182.

CALCU-DOKU

Use arithmetic and deductive logic to complete the grid so that each row and column contains the numbers 1 through 6 in some order. Numbers in each outlined set of squares combine to produce the number in the top corner using the mathematical sign indicated.

9+		5+		16+	
20×		3+			
2×	10×		24×	12×	
	2÷			4×	11+
15×		10×			
	10+			3+	

Answers on page 182.

SUDOKU

Use deductive logic to complete the grid so that each row, each column, and each 3 by 3 box contains the numbers 1 through 9 in some order. The solution is unique.

	9					4		
		7					3	
3	8					1	2	
9			5					6
		9	8	1				
2			3					1
	5	9					7	4
	7			8				
		6				9		

Answers on page 183.

SUDOKU

Use deductive logic to complete the grid so that each row, each column, and each 3 by 3 box contains the numbers 1 through 9 in some order. The solution is unique.

		4	1					8
	9					6	2	
		7			2			
8			2			9		
			4	3	1			
		5			6			7
			7			1		
	7	1					9	
6					3	4		

Answers on page 183.

SUDOKU

Use deductive logic to complete the grid so that each row, each column, and each 3 by 3 box contains the numbers 1 through 9 in some order. The solution is unique.

	8			4	7			
7	4							8
3						7		
	2	6	1		4			
			7					
			3		9	6	2	
		1						5
4							3	1
			9	2			8	

Answers on page 183.

SUDOKU

Use deductive logic to complete the grid so that each row, each column, and each 3 by 3 box contains the numbers 1 through 9 in some order. The solution is unique.

	3	5		8				
1				2	6			
4		2				5		
	6							5
			8	1	9			
7							1	
	9					8		1
			2	3				4
				4		7	5	

Answers on page 183.

SUDOKU

Use deductive logic to complete the grid so that each row, each column, and each 3 by 3 box contains the numbers 1 through 9 in some order. The solution is unique.

					6			9
		7						
3	8		7	5		4		
2		9	6					
7				1				3
					5	8		4
		1		8	7		4	2
						3		
6			5					

Answers on page 183.

SUDOKU

Use deductive logic to complete the grid so that each row, each column, and each 3 by 3 box contains the numbers 1 through 9 in some order. The solution is unique.

			2	1		6		5
		4		7				
			4			1		
5	8				3			
2				5				6
			6				5	1
		7			4			
				6		7		
9		1		3	2			

Answers on page 183.

ODD-EVEN LOGIDOKU

The numbers 1 through 9 appear once in every row, column, long diagonal, 3 by 3 grid, and irregular shape. Cells marked with the letter E contain even numbers. From the numbers already given, can you complete the puzzle?

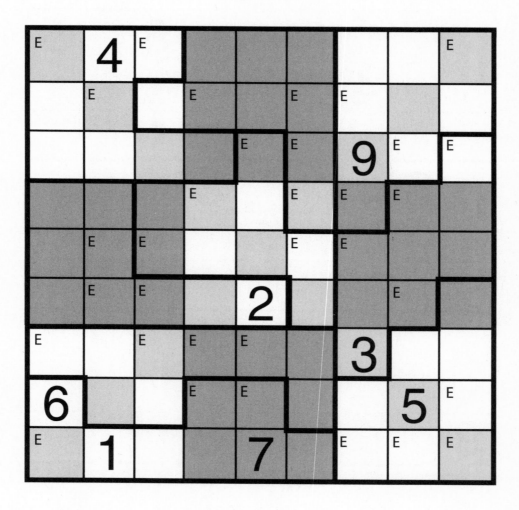

Answers on page 184.

SUDOKU

Use deductive logic to complete the grid so that each row, each column, and each 3 by 3 box contains the numbers 1 through 9 in some order. The solution is unique.

	1		3					8
					9	6	5	
7								
	8		2		6			5
	9			3			7	
6			7		1		9	
								3
	4	2	6					
9					4		8	

Answers on page 184.

SUDOKU

Use deductive logic to complete the grid so that each row, each column, and each 3 by 3 box contains the numbers 1 through 9 in some order. The solution is unique.

		7		9	8		5	
		4		6				
8			2				9	
1			3				7	
				1				
	2				9			3
	7				6			2
				7		6		
	9		1	8		4		

Answers on page 184.

SUDOKU

Use deductive logic to complete the grid so that each row, each column, and each 3 by 3 box contains the numbers 1 through 9 in some order. The solution is unique.

1					7		9	
		4				2		
			9		6	1	8	
		3					2	9
				5				
6	2					4		
	6	1	5		2			
		9				7		
	7		8					6

Answers on page 184.

SUDOKU

Use deductive logic to complete the grid so that each row, each column, and each 3 by 3 box contains the numbers 1 through 9 in some order. The solution is unique.

5		8	4					
			8				4	
7						5	9	
			7			3		2
3				5				4
2		7			8			
	6	1						9
	3				6			
					9	8		1

Answers on page 184.

SUDOKU

Use deductive logic to complete the grid so that each row, each column, and each 3 by 3 box contains the numbers 1 through 9 in some order. The solution is unique.

	9		2		7		1	
2								5
		1		4		9		
4								8
		6		9		2		
3								7
		3		7		4		
5								6
	2		1		5		8	

Answers on page 184.

CALCU-DOKU

Use arithmetic and deductive logic to complete the grid so that each row and column contains the numbers 1 through 6 in some order. Numbers in each outlined set of squares combine to produce the number in the top corner using the mathematical sign indicated.

11+		11+		6+	
15×	4×	20×	18×		
				3÷	
	6+		10+	6+	30×
5+	6×				
	6	3+		15×	

Answers on page 185.

SUDOKU

Use deductive logic to complete the grid so that each row, each column, and each 3 by 3 box contains the numbers 1 through 9 in some order. The solution is unique.

4			8					1
	7			3		2	9	
			5				3	
5		6						
	9			4			2	
						6		9
	8				1			
	3	5		6			4	
9					5			7

Answers on page 185.

SUDOKU

Use deductive logic to complete the grid so that each row, each column, and each 3 by 3 box contains the numbers 1 through 9 in some order. The solution is unique.

	4			1			3	
		8		9				
	5				6			
7		9		1		8		
9			5				3	
8		3		2		1		
	6				2			
		2		3				
5			8			6		

Answers on page 185.

SUDOKU

Use deductive logic to complete the grid so that each row, each column, and each 3 by 3 box contains the numbers 1 through 9 in some order. The solution is unique.

	8					1		
		5			8			3
2				7			8	
	6		7		9			
		1				2		
			8		4		7	
	9			3				6
1			2			3		
		4					1	

Answers on page 185.

SUDOKU

Use deductive logic to complete the grid so that each row, each column, and each 3 by 3 box contains the numbers 1 through 9 in some order. The solution is unique.

	1				8		7	
2		3	1			4		5
8			4		1		5	
				8				
	9		2		3			1
1		2			4	3		6
	3		9				8	

Answers on page 185.

SUDOKU

Use deductive logic to complete the grid so that each row, each column, and each 3 by 3 box contains the numbers 1 through 9 in some order. The solution is unique.

			1	2		6		
			5	4			7	
						3		2
7	9							
2	8			3			5	9
							2	7
6		2						
	3			7	8			
		9		1	2			

Answers on page 185.

SUDOKU

Use deductive logic to complete the grid so that each row, each column, and each 3 by 3 box contains the numbers 1 through 9 in some order. The solution is unique.

9			1	2				7
	1	6				8	4	
			2		9		7	
	9						1	
	8		5		4			
	4	1				5	9	
7				3	6			1

Answers on page 186.

ODD-EVEN LOGIDOKU

The numbers 1 through 9 appear once in every row, column, long diagonal, 3 by 3 grid, and irregular shape. Cells marked with the letter E contain even numbers. From the numbers already given, can you complete the puzzle?

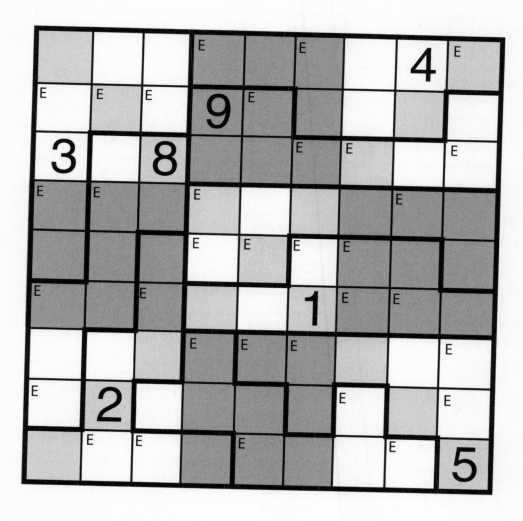

Answers on page 186.

SUDOKU

Use deductive logic to complete the grid so that each row, each column, and each 3 by 3 box contains the numbers 1 through 9 in some order. The solution is unique.

1								
			8				3	7
		7		5				8
			1				5	2
		5		2		8		
9	7				3			
2				6		1		
4	8				2			
								9

Answers on page 186.

SUDOKU

Use deductive logic to complete the grid so that each row, each column, and each 3 by 3 box contains the numbers 1 through 9 in some order. The solution is unique.

		5	7			6	1		
					8			
9			3					8
5	4					7		3
				3				
6		2					9	5
4					7			6
			2					
		8	1		9	2		

Answers on page 186.

SUDOKU

Use deductive logic to complete the grid so that each row, each column, and each 3 by 3 box contains the numbers 1 through 9 in some order. The solution is unique.

3	6						4	7
1			3		5			2
	2		7		4		5	
	9		5		2		6	
7			6		1			3
4	8						2	5

Answers on page 186.

SUDOKU

Use deductive logic to complete the grid so that each row, each column, and each 3 by 3 box contains the numbers 1 through 9 in some order. The solution is unique.

			1		8			
1								5
	8		6		5		7	
9		1				2		6
5		3				4		7
	3		8		1		5	
2								4
			7		9			

Answers on page 186.

SUDOKU

Use deductive logic to complete the grid so that each row, each column, and each 3 by 3 box contains the numbers 1 through 9 in some order. The solution is unique.

8						1		9
	4			5		6	8	
2	6							
		5		4				
	2						6	
			7		1			
							3	5
	3	5		4			1	
6		1						8

Answers on page 187.

CALCU-DOKU

Use arithmetic and deductive logic to complete the grid so that each row and column contains the numbers 1 through 6 in some order. Numbers in each outlined set of squares combine to produce the number in the top corner using the mathematical sign indicated.

5×	15×	8×		9+	
		20×	7+	3+	
10+				6+	15×
5+	6×	12×			
		4+	15×		
8×			12+		

Answers on page 187.

SUDOKU

Use deductive logic to complete the grid so that each row, each column, and each 3 by 3 box contains the numbers 1 through 9 in some order. The solution is unique.

8				6				3
		5	2			7		
	9		5				6	
				5		3	9	
7								5
	8	1		9				
	4				1		3	
		8			2	6		
1				3				4

Answers on page 187.

SUDOKU

Use deductive logic to complete the grid so that each row, each column, and each 3 by 3 box contains the numbers 1 through 9 in some order. The solution is unique.

	3						8	
4		2			6	1		7
			4					
	9		8	2	1	7		
		8	9	5	4		1	
					9			
5		6	1			8		3
	1						4	

Answers on page 187.

SUDOKU

Use deductive logic to complete the grid so that each row, each column, and each 3 by 3 box contains the numbers 1 through 9 in some order. The solution is unique.

	9		4		8		2	
	5						8	
8								7
1				6				8
			7	3	9			
9				1				3
3								9
	2						1	
	8		1		5		4	

Answers on page 187.

SUDOKU

Use deductive logic to complete the grid so that each row, each column, and each 3 by 3 box contains the numbers 1 through 9 in some order. The solution is unique.

			5		2			
		7	3		1	2		
	1						8	
5	6						7	4
				6				
3	4						6	5
	9						1	
		8	7		9	6		
			6		3			

Answers on page 187.

SUDOKU

Use deductive logic to complete the grid so that each row, each column, and each 3 by 3 box contains the numbers 1 through 9 in some order. The solution is unique.

	7						3	
3			6		8			1
		8				2		
5	8			6			2	3
2	1			3			8	5
		7				6		
4			1		9			2
	3						9	

Answers on page 188.

SUDOKU

Use deductive logic to complete the grid so that each row, each column, and each 3 by 3 box contains the numbers 1 through 9 in some order. The solution is unique.

							5		7
			2		4	8	1	
		7						2
2	6	3				4		
			8					
	8			5	1	3		
6						2		
	8	2	9		1			
5		4						

ODD-EVEN LOGIDOKU

The numbers 1 through 9 appear once in every row, column, long diagonal, 3 by 3 grid, and irregular shape. Cells marked with the letter E contain even numbers. From the numbers already given, can you complete the puzzle?

Answers on page 188.

SUDOKU

Use deductive logic to complete the grid so that each row, each column, and each 3 by 3 box contains the numbers 1 through 9 in some order. The solution is unique.

						6		2
5								7
			6	5			4	
7				4	2		9	
	6		9		1		3	
	8		3	6				4
	5			8	3			
6								1
1		9						

Answers on page 188.

SUDOKU

Use deductive logic to complete the grid so that each row, each column, and each 3 by 3 box contains the numbers 1 through 9 in some order. The solution is unique.

4			1		5			8
		3		7		6		
5			7		2			9
		2		1		7		
3			9		4			2
		1		4		3		
9			5		8			7

Answers on page 188.

SUDOKU

Use deductive logic to complete the grid so that each row, each column, and each 3 by 3 box contains the numbers 1 through 9 in some order. The solution is unique.

				7	3			
2						3	6	
9		8		6				
	7					8	1	
			4	3	7			
	6	4					7	
				9		2		5
	2	6						1
			7	1				

Answers on page 188.

SUDOKU

Use deductive logic to complete the grid so that each row, each column, and each 3 by 3 box contains the numbers 1 through 9 in some order. The solution is unique.

			6					
5					2			1
8	7			1			9	4
	3			2				8
		2				4		
4				9			7	
7	2			5			4	9
9			7					5
					9			

Answers on page 189.

SUDOKU

Use deductive logic to complete the grid so that each row, each column, and each 3 by 3 box contains the numbers 1 through 9 in some order. The solution is unique.

	4		1		2		6	
6	7						4	9
8			2		7			6
				9				
9			3		6			7
1	5						8	2
	3		6		8		7	

Answers on page 189.

CALCU-DOKU

Use arithmetic and deductive logic to complete the grid so that each row and column contains the numbers 1 through 5 in some order. Numbers in each outlined set of squares combine to produce the number in the top corner using the mathematical sign indicated.

5+	4+	5	6×	
		9+		
12×		2×		20×
10×	5×		7+	
	5+			

Answers on page 189.

SUDOKU

Use deductive logic to complete the grid so that each row, each column, and each 3 by 3 box contains the numbers 1 through 9 in some order. The solution is unique.

2			7		5			3
	6						8	
			4		1			
8		9				4		6
1		4				7		5
			1		8			
	8						2	
5			3		4			9

Answers on page 189.

SUDOKU

Use deductive logic to complete the grid so that each row, each column, and each 3 by 3 box contains the numbers 1 through 9 in some order. The solution is unique.

	3							
2	4		1					
		5				8		2
		1	9	3		2		
	6		8		4		7	
		8		2	5	4		
9		4				1		
					1		5	6
							2	

Answers on page 189.

SUDOKU

Use deductive logic to complete the grid so that each row, each column, and each 3 by 3 box contains the numbers 1 through 9 in some order. The solution is unique.

	9			5		3	8	
7		8			2			5
							1	
					7			6
			6	3	5			
9			4					
	7							
5			9			8		4
	1	9		6			2	

Answers on page 189.

SUDOKU

Use deductive logic to complete the grid so that each row, each column, and each 3 by 3 box contains the numbers 1 through 9 in some order. The solution is unique.

			2					
	2			8		4	5	9
4	6				3			
2		1						
	4						2	
						5		6
			4				1	5
1	5	9		3			4	
					7			

Answers on page 190.

SUDOKU

Use deductive logic to complete the grid so that each row, each column, and each 3 by 3 box contains the numbers 1 through 9 in some order. The solution is unique.

				9			7	4
		6	1					3
	5				6			
	8		2			4		
5								9
		3			8		6	
			8				1	
7					2	9		
2	4			3				

Answers on page 190.

SUDOKU

Use deductive logic to complete the grid so that each row, each column, and each 3 by 3 box contains the numbers 1 through 9 in some order. The solution is unique.

5						4		9
		3	7				5	2
	9	6			4			
			1			2		
	8		5		6		3	
		4			8			
			9			7	1	
	6				1	8		
3		2						4

Answers on page 190.

ODD-EVEN LOGIDOKU

The numbers 1 through 9 appear once in every row, column, long diagonal, 3 by 3 grid, and irregular shape. Cells marked with the letter E contain even numbers. From the numbers already given, can you complete the puzzle?

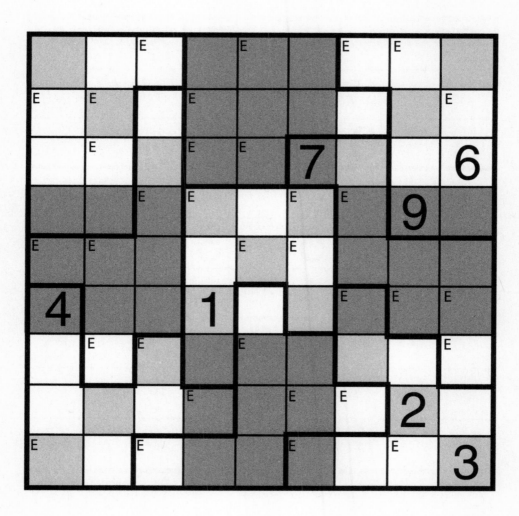

Answers on page 190.

SUDOKU

Use deductive logic to complete the grid so that each row, each column, and each 3 by 3 box contains the numbers 1 through 9 in some order. The solution is unique.

2					7	5		
				5			8	
5		6					9	
1				4				
	9	5	7	3	2			
		1						3
	7					3		6
	6		8					
	1	3						9

Answers on page 190.

SUDOKU

Use deductive logic to complete the grid so that each row, each column, and each 3 by 3 box contains the numbers 1 through 9 in some order. The solution is unique.

						1		9
					1		6	
2		6		4	5			
4	2						9	6
		1				5		
5	3						8	1
			7	8		2		4
	9		2					
1		2						

Answers on page 190.

SUDOKU

Use deductive logic to complete the grid so that each row, each column, and each 3 by 3 box contains the numbers 1 through 9 in some order. The solution is unique.

		5			8			7
					4		8	
3				5		9		
					9		4	1
		7				5		
8	9		1					
		6		9				2
	1		2					
2			7			6		

Answers on page 191.

SUDOKU

Use deductive logic to complete the grid so that each row, each column, and each 3 by 3 box contains the numbers 1 through 9 in some order. The solution is unique.

		8		7				
		5	9			3		
	4				1		6	9
		6					9	
1								5
	8					2		
3	6		4				7	
		7			8	6		
				2		4		

Answers on page 191.

SUDOKU

Use deductive logic to complete the grid so that each row, each column, and each 3 by 3 box contains the numbers 1 through 9 in some order. The solution is unique.

2				4				8
	1				9	7		
					7		9	
			3			4	1	
1								9
	2	7			6			
	3		7					
		8	2				5	
5				9				4

Answers on page 191.

CALCU-DOKU

Use arithmetic and deductive logic to complete the grid so that each row and column contains the numbers 1 through 6 in some order. Numbers in each outlined set of squares combine to produce the number in the top corner using the mathematical sign indicated.

1−		3×		10+	
3÷		5	4		
3×	5×		10+		2
	6+		5+	30×	
2÷	4+	15+		6×	15×

Answers on page 191.

SUDOKU

Use deductive logic to complete the grid so that each row, each column, and each 3 by 3 box contains the numbers 1 through 9 in some order. The solution is unique.

		5	8					6
	3	2	6					
				4			9	
5					4			
	7	4		5		9	6	
			3					5
	9			1				
					8	7	5	
4					3	1		

Answers on page 191.

SUDOKU

Use deductive logic to complete the grid so that each row, each column, and each 3 by 3 box contains the numbers 1 through 9 in some order. The solution is unique.

			1				4	
	1				4		5	
5						3	9	
		2			1			7
4				7				3
8			2			4		
	2	8						9
	4		6				2	
	9				5			

Answers on page 191.

SUDOKU

Use deductive logic to complete the grid so that each row, each column, and each 3 by 3 box contains the numbers 1 through 9 in some order. The solution is unique.

5	6			2				9
							3	7
			5	7				
8					4			
	7	5				4	6	
		9						3
			6	2				
4	2							
6			9				2	1

Answers on page 192.

SUDOKU

Use deductive logic to complete the grid so that each row, each column, and each 3 by 3 box contains the numbers 1 through 9 in some order. The solution is unique.

	5			9				6
	1						9	
			1				3	7
7		9	3					
		8		4		6		
					8	2		9
6	3				7			
	9						4	
1				5			6	

Answers on page 192.

SUDOKU

Use deductive logic to complete the grid so that each row, each column, and each 3 by 3 box contains the numbers 1 through 9 in some order. The solution is unique.

	8				1			
	2		9	3				6
		4					5	
	3			9				8
2								4
7				5			3	
	6					2		
4				1	5		7	
			2				1	

Answers on page 192.

SUDOKU

Use deductive logic to complete the grid so that each row, each column, and each 3 by 3 box contains the numbers 1 through 9 in some order. The solution is unique.

			8		6		7	
8								
9	3				2			5
1		9			3			
	6	8				9	1	
			6			3		8
5			4				6	2
								1
	4		3		8		5	

Answers on page 192.

ODD-EVEN LOGIDOKU

The numbers 1 through 9 appear once in every row, column, long diagonal, 3 by 3 grid, and irregular shape. Cells marked with the letter E contain even numbers. From the numbers already given, can you complete the puzzle?

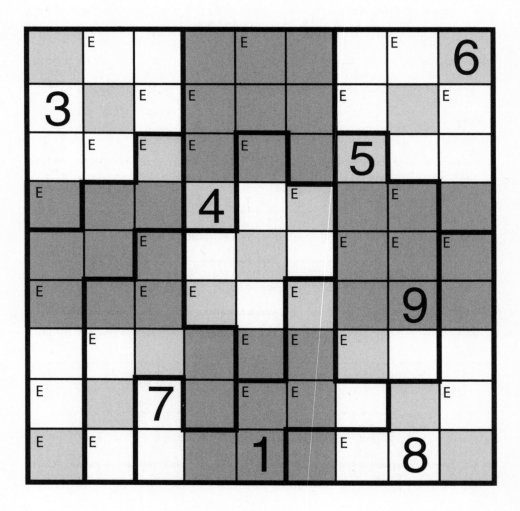

Answers on page 192.

SUDOKU

Use deductive logic to complete the grid so that each row, each column, and each 3 by 3 box contains the numbers 1 through 9 in some order. The solution is unique.

	2	3	7			4		
					1			8
7					8			6
	5	2						9
9						8	6	
2			5					4
4			2					
		8			3	1	9	

Answers on page 192.

ANSWERS

SUDOKU (page 3)

7	4	5	2	1	6	8	9	3
9	3	2	8	7	4	5	6	1
6	1	8	5	9	3	2	4	7
4	9	7	6	8	5	1	3	2
8	6	1	9	3	2	7	5	4
5	2	3	1	4	7	6	8	9
2	7	6	3	5	9	4	1	8
1	5	9	4	2	8	3	7	6
3	8	4	7	6	1	9	2	5

SUDOKU (page 4)

7	5	1	3	2	4	9	6	8
4	6	3	8	9	1	5	2	7
9	8	2	5	6	7	1	4	3
6	1	7	2	4	5	3	8	9
5	4	8	9	7	3	6	1	2
2	3	9	6	1	8	4	7	5
1	9	4	7	3	2	8	5	6
3	2	5	4	8	6	7	9	1
8	7	6	1	5	9	2	3	4

SUDOKU (page 5)

3	2	4	1	6	5	9	8	7
7	1	6	9	8	2	4	3	5
9	8	5	4	7	3	1	6	2
2	6	1	3	4	8	5	7	9
4	3	7	5	9	1	6	2	8
8	5	9	6	2	7	3	1	4
5	7	3	8	1	4	2	9	6
1	9	2	7	5	6	8	4	3
6	4	8	2	3	9	7	5	1

SUDOKU (page 6)

4	8	3	6	9	7	1	5	2
1	2	5	4	8	3	6	9	7
7	9	6	1	2	5	3	4	8
6	3	2	7	5	1	4	8	9
9	7	4	2	3	8	5	1	6
8	5	1	9	6	4	2	7	3
2	1	7	8	4	6	9	3	5
3	4	9	5	7	2	8	6	1
5	6	8	3	1	9	7	2	4

SUDOKU (page 7)

5	6	9	2	8	4	7	3	1
4	3	8	9	1	7	5	2	6
2	7	1	3	6	5	8	4	9
7	4	2	5	9	1	6	8	3
6	1	3	7	4	8	2	9	5
8	9	5	6	2	3	4	1	7
3	8	7	4	5	9	1	6	2
1	5	6	8	3	2	9	7	4
9	2	4	1	7	6	3	5	8

SUDOKU (page 8)

1	5	6	8	9	2	3	7	4
2	4	8	7	1	3	6	9	5
9	3	7	6	4	5	2	8	1
7	6	9	2	3	1	5	4	8
5	8	4	9	6	7	1	2	3
3	1	2	4	5	8	7	6	9
4	9	5	1	2	6	8	3	7
6	7	3	5	8	9	4	1	2
8	2	1	3	7	4	9	5	6

ANSWERS

LOGIDOKU (page 9)

7	9	2	3	5	1	6	8	4
5	6	1	9	4	8	7	2	3
3	4	8	2	7	6	5	1	9
4	8	6	5	1	7	9	3	2
1	2	7	8	3	9	4	5	6
9	3	5	6	2	4	1	7	8
6	7	9	1	8	3	2	4	5
2	1	3	4	6	5	8	9	7
8	5	4	7	9	2	3	6	1

SUDOKU (page 12)

4	5	3	2	9	6	7	1	8
9	2	7	1	3	8	6	4	5
1	8	6	7	4	5	9	2	3
2	7	5	6	1	3	8	9	4
3	4	9	8	7	2	1	5	6
6	1	8	4	5	9	2	3	7
5	9	2	3	6	7	4	8	1
7	3	1	9	8	4	5	6	2
8	6	4	5	2	1	3	7	9

SUDOKU (page 10)

1	9	5	3	8	4	7	6	2
3	4	6	7	9	2	8	5	1
7	8	2	1	6	5	4	3	9
6	1	3	5	2	8	9	4	7
5	2	9	4	1	7	6	8	3
8	7	4	6	3	9	2	1	5
4	3	1	2	7	6	5	9	8
9	5	7	8	4	3	1	2	6
2	6	8	9	5	1	3	7	4

SUDOKU (page 13)

1	9	3	2	8	4	5	6	7
7	4	6	9	1	5	3	2	8
5	8	2	3	6	7	4	1	9
4	5	7	8	9	2	1	3	6
9	6	8	4	3	1	7	5	2
2	3	1	5	7	6	9	8	4
8	1	5	6	4	9	2	7	3
3	7	4	1	2	8	6	9	5
6	2	9	7	5	3	8	4	1

SUDOKU (page 11)

6	5	1	9	8	7	3	4	2
3	4	7	2	6	5	8	9	1
2	8	9	1	3	4	5	6	7
7	1	2	6	4	3	9	8	5
4	3	5	8	1	9	2	7	6
9	6	8	7	5	2	4	1	3
5	2	6	4	7	8	1	3	9
1	9	4	3	2	6	7	5	8
8	7	3	5	9	1	6	2	4

SUDOKU (page 14)

6	5	3	1	9	2	8	7	4
1	4	2	7	8	6	5	9	3
9	7	8	4	3	5	2	6	1
2	6	7	8	4	3	1	5	9
3	8	5	2	1	9	6	4	7
4	1	9	6	5	7	3	8	2
8	9	6	3	2	4	7	1	5
5	2	1	9	7	8	4	3	6
7	3	4	5	6	1	9	2	8

ANSWERS

SUDOKU (page 15)

9	2	3	7	4	5	6	8	1
5	1	7	2	6	8	9	3	4
6	8	4	1	9	3	2	7	5
2	4	8	9	5	7	3	1	6
7	6	1	4	3	2	8	5	9
3	9	5	6	8	1	4	2	7
4	5	2	8	7	6	1	9	3
8	7	9	3	1	4	5	6	2
1	3	6	5	2	9	7	4	8

CALCU-DOKU (page 16)

3	1	5	2	4
2	5	4	3	1
4	2	3	1	5
1	4	2	5	3
5	3	1	4	2

SUDOKU (page 17)

7	4	2	1	6	9	8	5	3
9	5	1	2	8	3	4	6	7
6	8	3	7	4	5	2	1	9
8	9	6	4	5	1	3	7	2
1	2	5	3	9	7	6	8	4
4	3	7	8	2	6	5	9	1
5	6	4	9	1	2	7	3	8
3	1	8	6	7	4	9	2	5
2	7	9	5	3	8	1	4	6

SUDOKU (page 18)

5	8	1	2	6	4	9	7	3
2	6	9	1	7	3	5	4	8
3	4	7	8	5	9	1	2	6
4	9	3	6	2	8	7	5	1
6	5	2	7	3	1	4	8	9
7	1	8	9	4	5	3	6	2
1	7	5	3	8	6	2	9	4
9	2	6	4	1	7	8	3	5
8	3	4	5	9	2	6	1	7

SUDOKU (page 19)

7	2	8	3	4	6	1	9	5
6	4	1	2	9	5	7	8	3
9	5	3	7	8	1	4	2	6
3	1	7	5	6	9	8	4	2
2	9	6	8	3	4	5	1	7
4	8	5	1	7	2	6	3	9
1	3	4	6	2	7	9	5	8
8	6	9	4	5	3	2	7	1
5	7	2	9	1	8	3	6	4

SUDOKU (page 20)

5	4	1	2	9	7	8	6	3
2	7	8	1	3	6	4	9	5
9	3	6	4	8	5	1	7	2
8	6	3	9	5	2	7	4	1
1	2	7	6	4	8	5	3	9
4	9	5	3	7	1	6	2	8
7	1	4	5	2	9	3	8	6
6	8	2	7	1	3	9	5	4
3	5	9	8	6	4	2	1	7

LOGIDOKU (page 21)

5	6	1	2	9	8	3	7	4
3	8	9	7	4	6	5	2	1
4	7	2	5	3	1	8	6	9
1	2	3	9	8	5	7	4	6
7	4	8	6	1	2	9	5	3
9	5	6	3	7	4	1	8	2
8	3	7	4	2	9	6	1	5
2	9	5	1	6	7	4	3	8
6	1	4	8	5	3	2	9	7

ANSWERS

SUDOKU (page 22)

2	1	8	5	6	7	3	9	4
4	7	9	8	3	2	6	5	1
5	6	3	4	1	9	7	8	2
6	8	5	3	2	4	9	1	7
7	3	2	1	9	6	5	4	8
1	9	4	7	8	5	2	6	3
9	2	7	6	4	8	1	3	5
8	5	1	9	7	3	4	2	6
3	4	6	2	5	1	8	7	9

SUDOKU (page 25)

5	3	9	7	1	8	2	6	4
7	8	2	5	4	6	1	3	9
6	4	1	2	9	3	5	7	8
3	2	5	6	8	4	9	1	7
1	6	8	3	7	9	4	5	2
4	9	7	1	2	5	3	8	6
2	7	3	9	6	1	8	4	5
8	5	6	4	3	2	7	9	1
9	1	4	8	5	7	6	2	3

SUDOKU (page 23)

4	3	5	6	9	1	8	7	2
8	2	1	7	4	3	9	6	5
6	9	7	8	5	2	4	1	3
7	6	9	4	8	5	3	2	1
3	1	4	9	2	6	7	5	8
2	5	8	3	1	7	6	4	9
5	7	3	2	6	9	1	8	4
9	8	2	1	7	4	5	3	6
1	4	6	5	3	8	2	9	7

SUDOKU (page 26)

1	5	8	7	4	9	2	3	6
6	4	3	2	8	5	1	9	7
9	7	2	3	1	6	5	8	4
5	8	1	4	3	2	7	6	9
3	9	6	8	5	7	4	1	2
7	2	4	9	6	1	8	5	3
4	6	9	1	2	8	3	7	5
8	3	7	5	9	4	6	2	1
2	1	5	6	7	3	9	4	8

SUDOKU (page 24)

9	4	2	7	8	3	1	5	6
6	7	8	1	5	4	3	2	9
1	3	5	9	6	2	8	4	7
7	8	6	2	3	1	5	9	4
2	1	4	5	9	8	6	7	3
3	5	9	6	4	7	2	1	8
8	9	7	3	1	5	4	6	2
5	2	3	4	7	6	9	8	1
4	6	1	8	2	9	7	3	5

CALCU-DOKU (page 27)

5	1	3	4	2
3	4	2	1	5
4	3	5	2	1
1	2	4	5	3
2	5	1	3	4

ANSWERS

SUDOKU (page 28)

7	4	5	8	9	6	2	3	1
8	3	1	5	2	7	4	9	6
9	2	6	3	1	4	7	8	5
5	6	3	1	4	9	8	2	7
1	9	2	7	5	8	3	6	4
4	7	8	2	6	3	5	1	9
3	1	9	4	7	2	6	5	8
2	5	4	6	8	1	9	7	3
6	8	7	9	3	5	1	4	2

SUDOKU (page 31)

6	2	8	5	3	7	4	9	1
7	9	1	6	4	2	8	5	3
5	4	3	8	9	1	2	6	7
1	3	2	7	8	9	6	4	5
4	7	9	3	6	5	1	2	8
8	6	5	1	2	4	3	7	9
9	1	4	2	5	3	7	8	6
3	5	6	4	7	8	9	1	2
2	8	7	9	1	6	5	3	4

SUDOKU (page 29)

7	6	4	3	1	8	9	2	5
3	9	8	2	5	6	7	4	1
2	5	1	4	9	7	3	6	8
4	3	6	5	2	1	8	7	9
5	2	7	8	4	9	6	1	3
8	1	9	7	6	3	2	5	4
6	7	3	1	8	4	5	9	2
9	4	2	6	3	5	1	8	7
1	8	5	9	7	2	4	3	6

SUDOKU (page 32)

8	1	3	2	4	7	9	6	5
5	9	6	3	8	1	7	4	2
4	2	7	5	6	9	1	8	3
2	7	5	6	9	3	4	1	8
3	4	8	7	1	2	6	5	9
9	6	1	4	5	8	3	2	7
7	5	2	1	3	4	8	9	6
1	3	9	8	2	6	5	7	4
6	8	4	9	7	5	2	3	1

SUDOKU (page 30)

8	9	3	5	7	2	1	6	4
6	7	4	9	1	8	2	5	3
2	1	5	6	4	3	7	8	9
3	5	9	7	2	4	8	1	6
7	8	6	3	5	1	4	9	2
1	4	2	8	9	6	5	3	7
4	3	7	1	8	9	6	2	5
5	6	1	2	3	7	9	4	8
9	2	8	4	6	5	3	7	1

SUDOKU (page 33)

2	3	1	8	5	7	6	9	4
6	4	7	9	2	1	5	3	8
9	5	8	4	3	6	1	7	2
3	8	6	2	1	9	4	5	7
1	7	9	6	4	5	2	8	3
5	2	4	3	7	8	9	1	6
8	6	5	7	9	2	3	4	1
4	1	2	5	8	3	7	6	9
7	9	3	1	6	4	8	2	5

ANSWERS

LOGIDOKU (page 34)

2	6	9	5	8	3	1	4	7
7	8	1	4	2	9	5	6	3
4	3	5	1	6	7	2	9	8
8	7	2	6	3	5	9	1	4
1	9	6	8	4	2	3	7	5
5	4	3	9	7	1	6	8	2
6	5	8	3	9	4	7	2	1
9	1	7	2	5	8	4	3	6
3	2	4	7	1	6	8	5	9

SUDOKU (page 37)

2	7	5	4	9	3	1	6	8
1	4	9	2	6	8	5	3	7
6	8	3	1	7	5	4	2	9
9	1	8	6	4	2	3	7	5
4	3	7	5	8	1	6	9	2
5	6	2	9	3	7	8	4	1
7	2	6	8	1	4	9	5	3
8	5	4	3	2	9	7	1	6
3	9	1	7	5	6	2	8	4

SUDOKU (page 35)

8	6	9	3	7	1	2	5	4
1	2	4	8	6	5	3	7	9
5	3	7	2	4	9	6	8	1
3	7	1	9	5	6	8	4	2
2	9	8	1	3	4	7	6	5
6	4	5	7	2	8	1	9	3
4	1	6	5	8	3	9	2	7
7	8	3	4	9	2	5	1	6
9	5	2	6	1	7	4	3	8

SUDOKU (page 38)

5	9	7	3	4	1	2	6	8
4	2	3	6	8	7	9	5	1
6	1	8	9	2	5	7	3	4
1	3	5	8	7	4	6	9	2
2	8	6	5	9	3	1	4	7
9	7	4	2	1	6	3	8	5
8	4	2	1	6	9	5	7	3
3	6	1	7	5	8	4	2	9
7	5	9	4	3	2	8	1	6

SUDOKU (page 36)

6	3	1	9	2	7	5	4	8
5	7	8	6	4	1	3	2	9
9	2	4	8	5	3	6	1	7
2	8	7	3	6	4	9	5	1
3	1	9	5	7	8	2	6	4
4	5	6	1	9	2	8	7	3
7	6	2	4	3	9	1	8	5
1	4	3	2	8	5	7	9	6
8	9	5	7	1	6	4	3	2

SUDOKU (page 39)

7	6	4	2	9	8	3	1	5
1	3	8	6	5	7	2	4	9
2	9	5	3	1	4	8	6	7
5	4	3	8	7	6	1	9	2
6	7	9	1	2	3	4	5	8
8	1	2	9	4	5	6	7	3
4	8	1	7	3	9	5	2	6
9	2	6	5	8	1	7	3	4
3	5	7	4	6	2	9	8	1

ANSWERS

CALCU-DOKU (page 40)

2	4	3	1	5
4	1	5	2	3
1	5	4	3	2
5	3	2	4	1
3	2	1	5	4

SUDOKU (page 43)

3	8	4	7	9	1	6	5	2
7	1	9	6	2	5	8	3	4
5	6	2	4	3	8	1	9	7
4	2	3	5	1	6	7	8	9
1	5	7	2	8	9	3	4	6
6	9	8	3	4	7	5	2	1
2	7	5	9	6	3	4	1	8
9	3	1	8	7	4	2	6	5
8	4	6	1	5	2	9	7	3

SUDOKU (page 41)

9	6	5	8	7	3	4	2	1
4	8	1	6	2	9	3	7	5
3	2	7	1	5	4	8	6	9
7	3	6	9	8	1	2	5	4
8	4	2	7	6	5	1	9	3
1	5	9	3	4	2	7	8	6
2	7	3	5	1	6	9	4	8
6	1	4	2	9	8	5	3	7
5	9	8	4	3	7	6	1	2

SUDOKU (page 44)

1	9	4	3	7	5	6	8	2
3	5	8	1	2	6	7	4	9
6	7	2	9	8	4	1	3	5
2	6	3	7	1	9	4	5	8
8	4	7	5	6	3	9	2	1
9	1	5	2	4	8	3	7	6
5	8	6	4	9	7	2	1	3
4	3	1	6	5	2	8	9	7
7	2	9	8	3	1	5	6	4

SUDOKU (page 42)

1	9	2	3	6	5	8	4	7
4	3	6	7	8	9	2	5	1
5	8	7	1	2	4	3	9	6
6	2	1	8	4	7	5	3	9
8	5	9	2	3	6	1	7	4
7	4	3	9	5	1	6	8	2
3	1	8	4	9	2	7	6	5
9	7	5	6	1	3	4	2	8
2	6	4	5	7	8	9	1	3

SUDOKU (page 45)

5	1	8	7	6	9	3	2	4
3	6	9	4	2	8	5	7	1
7	2	4	5	3	1	8	6	9
1	8	3	2	9	7	6	4	5
2	7	5	8	4	6	9	1	3
4	9	6	3	1	5	2	8	7
9	5	2	1	8	4	7	3	6
8	4	7	6	5	3	1	9	2
6	3	1	9	7	2	4	5	8

ANSWERS

SUDOKU (page 46)

9	4	7	1	6	2	5	3	8
1	6	2	8	3	5	9	7	4
5	3	8	7	9	4	6	2	1
4	1	3	2	8	9	7	6	5
7	2	6	5	4	1	3	8	9
8	5	9	3	7	6	1	4	2
3	7	5	4	1	8	2	9	6
6	8	1	9	2	3	4	5	7
2	9	4	6	5	7	8	1	3

SUDOKU (page 49)

7	9	2	4	1	3	6	8	5
1	8	5	2	6	7	3	4	9
4	6	3	8	5	9	1	2	7
2	4	1	6	7	5	8	9	3
6	3	7	9	4	8	5	1	2
8	5	9	1	3	2	7	6	4
9	7	8	3	2	1	4	5	6
3	2	6	5	8	4	9	7	1
5	1	4	7	9	6	2	3	8

LOGIDOKU (page 47)

3	2	8	9	6	5	1	4	7
7	9	6	3	1	4	5	2	8
1	5	4	7	2	8	6	3	9
6	4	1	2	3	9	7	8	5
8	3	9	6	5	7	4	1	2
2	7	5	8	4	1	9	6	3
5	6	3	4	7	2	8	9	1
9	1	2	5	8	6	3	7	4
4	8	7	1	9	3	2	5	6

SUDOKU (page 50)

1	9	5	8	2	4	6	7	3
8	3	4	6	1	7	2	5	9
7	2	6	3	5	9	8	4	1
3	5	1	9	8	6	7	2	4
4	6	8	1	7	2	9	3	5
2	7	9	5	4	3	1	8	6
5	1	3	2	9	8	4	6	7
6	4	2	7	3	1	5	9	8
9	8	7	4	6	5	3	1	2

SUDOKU (page 48)

7	2	9	6	4	1	8	5	3
5	6	8	2	7	3	9	1	4
4	1	3	5	8	9	2	6	7
6	7	4	1	5	8	3	9	2
3	5	2	9	6	7	4	8	1
8	9	1	3	2	4	5	7	6
1	3	7	8	9	2	6	4	5
2	8	6	4	1	5	7	3	9
9	4	5	7	3	6	1	2	8

SUDOKU (page 51)

6	2	7	5	1	9	8	4	3
1	3	4	6	2	8	5	7	9
5	9	8	4	7	3	1	6	2
8	5	3	7	6	1	2	9	4
9	7	2	3	4	5	6	8	1
4	1	6	8	9	2	7	3	5
3	6	9	1	5	7	4	2	8
7	8	1	2	3	4	9	5	6
2	4	5	9	8	6	3	1	7

ANSWERS

SUDOKU (page 52)

2	3	8	7	1	9	5	4	6
5	9	1	4	2	6	3	8	7
7	6	4	5	3	8	2	9	1
6	4	2	1	7	3	9	5	8
8	1	9	6	5	2	7	3	4
3	7	5	8	9	4	6	1	2
9	2	6	3	8	1	4	7	5
1	5	3	2	4	7	8	6	9
4	8	7	9	6	5	1	2	3

SUDOKU (page 55)

7	2	6	1	3	5	9	4	8
9	5	8	4	2	7	3	1	6
3	1	4	9	6	8	2	5	7
2	8	1	7	5	4	6	3	9
6	7	9	8	1	3	5	2	4
5	4	3	2	9	6	7	8	1
1	6	2	5	4	9	8	7	3
8	3	5	6	7	1	4	9	2
4	9	7	3	8	2	1	6	5

CALCU-DOKU (page 53)

1	3	4	2
2	1	3	4
3	4	2	1
4	2	1	3

SUDOKU (page 56)

2	8	7	3	1	9	6	4	5
5	9	1	4	6	2	7	8	3
3	6	4	5	7	8	2	9	1
6	4	5	1	2	7	8	3	9
7	3	9	6	8	5	4	1	2
1	2	8	9	4	3	5	7	6
9	5	6	7	3	4	1	2	8
4	1	2	8	9	6	3	5	7
8	7	3	2	5	1	9	6	4

SUDOKU (page 54)

3	5	4	6	7	1	9	2	8
6	8	1	5	9	2	7	4	3
2	9	7	3	4	8	1	5	6
1	2	5	8	6	7	4	3	9
4	7	9	2	5	3	6	8	1
8	3	6	4	1	9	5	7	2
5	6	2	9	8	4	3	1	7
7	4	8	1	3	6	2	9	5
9	1	3	7	2	5	8	6	4

SUDOKU (page 57)

3	5	4	7	1	8	6	2	9
2	7	1	9	6	5	8	4	3
9	8	6	2	3	4	5	7	1
8	6	7	1	5	3	4	9	2
5	1	2	4	7	9	3	8	6
4	3	9	6	8	2	7	1	5
1	2	3	5	4	7	9	6	8
6	4	8	3	9	1	2	5	7
7	9	5	8	2	6	1	3	4

ANSWERS

SUDOKU (page 58)

8	4	9	6	3	1	2	5	7
7	6	1	2	5	9	3	4	8
3	5	2	7	8	4	1	6	9
2	3	4	9	6	8	5	7	1
1	9	6	5	7	2	4	8	3
5	7	8	1	4	3	9	2	6
4	8	5	3	9	7	6	1	2
6	1	3	8	2	5	7	9	4
9	2	7	4	1	6	8	3	5

SUDOKU (page 61)

9	3	2	1	4	8	5	6	7
7	4	8	3	5	6	9	2	1
5	1	6	7	9	2	3	8	4
8	5	4	6	3	7	1	9	2
1	2	3	9	8	5	7	4	6
6	7	9	2	1	4	8	3	5
4	6	5	8	7	9	2	1	3
2	8	1	5	6	3	4	7	9
3	9	7	4	2	1	6	5	8

SUDOKU (page 59)

3	1	6	5	2	4	7	8	9
4	9	7	8	3	6	5	1	2
5	8	2	1	9	7	4	6	3
7	4	8	6	1	3	9	2	5
1	2	3	9	4	5	6	7	8
9	6	5	2	7	8	1	3	4
2	5	1	7	8	9	3	4	6
6	7	4	3	5	2	8	9	1
8	3	9	4	6	1	2	5	7

SUDOKU (page 62)

9	7	2	1	3	8	5	4	6
6	3	1	5	4	7	9	8	2
4	8	5	2	6	9	3	7	1
5	1	6	4	7	3	2	9	8
7	4	8	9	1	2	6	5	3
2	9	3	8	5	6	7	1	4
8	2	7	3	9	4	1	6	5
3	5	9	6	8	1	4	2	7
1	6	4	7	2	5	8	3	9

LOGIDOKU (page 60)

5	7	3	9	1	4	8	6	2
6	4	2	3	8	7	5	9	1
8	1	9	6	5	2	7	3	4
4	9	5	7	2	3	1	8	6
3	8	7	5	6	1	4	2	9
2	6	1	4	9	8	3	7	5
9	3	8	1	4	6	2	5	7
7	5	4	2	3	9	6	1	8
1	2	6	8	7	5	9	4	3

SUDOKU (page 63)

9	7	2	5	4	3	6	8	1
4	3	5	8	6	1	9	7	2
8	1	6	9	2	7	3	4	5
3	5	8	2	9	6	4	1	7
2	6	4	7	1	5	8	9	3
1	9	7	3	8	4	2	5	6
5	2	3	4	7	8	1	6	9
7	8	1	6	3	9	5	2	4
6	4	9	1	5	2	7	3	8

ANSWERS

SUDOKU (page 64)

6	9	7	4	3	5	1	8	2
8	2	1	9	7	6	4	5	3
5	4	3	1	8	2	6	9	7
3	6	8	5	2	9	7	1	4
4	5	2	7	1	8	3	6	9
1	7	9	3	6	4	5	2	8
2	8	4	6	5	7	9	3	1
7	1	6	8	9	3	2	4	5
9	3	5	2	4	1	8	7	6

CALCU-DOKU (page 67)

2	4	1	3	5
5	3	4	2	1
4	5	2	1	3
3	1	5	4	2
1	2	3	5	4

SUDOKU (page 65)

5	7	2	6	9	1	4	3	8
1	6	8	5	3	4	7	2	9
9	3	4	8	7	2	5	6	1
4	1	9	7	2	8	3	5	6
6	5	3	1	4	9	8	7	2
2	8	7	3	5	6	1	9	4
3	2	1	9	8	5	6	4	7
8	9	5	4	6	7	2	1	3
7	4	6	2	1	3	9	8	5

SUDOKU (page 68)

9	5	8	3	2	1	7	4	6
6	4	3	7	5	9	1	8	2
1	2	7	4	8	6	3	9	5
5	1	4	9	3	8	2	6	7
8	7	9	6	1	2	4	5	3
2	3	6	5	4	7	8	1	9
4	6	1	2	7	5	9	3	8
7	8	5	1	9	3	6	2	4
3	9	2	8	6	4	5	7	1

SUDOKU (page 66)

3	7	6	1	9	8	5	4	2
5	4	9	2	6	7	1	8	3
1	2	8	4	5	3	7	6	9
7	3	4	5	2	9	6	1	8
9	8	1	6	7	4	3	2	5
2	6	5	3	8	1	4	9	7
6	9	3	8	4	5	2	7	1
8	1	2	7	3	6	9	5	4
4	5	7	9	1	2	8	3	6

SUDOKU (page 69)

2	3	8	6	4	1	9	7	5
1	5	4	9	7	8	6	2	3
7	9	6	2	3	5	1	4	8
3	4	7	8	9	6	5	1	2
5	2	9	3	1	4	7	8	6
8	6	1	7	5	2	4	3	9
4	1	2	5	8	9	3	6	7
9	8	3	1	6	7	2	5	4
6	7	5	4	2	3	8	9	1

ANSWERS

SUDOKU (page 70)

1	8	2	5	4	7	6	3	9
6	3	4	8	2	9	5	7	1
9	7	5	3	6	1	2	4	8
3	1	7	4	9	5	8	2	6
2	5	8	7	1	6	3	9	4
4	6	9	2	3	8	7	1	5
8	2	3	1	5	4	9	6	7
7	9	1	6	8	2	4	5	3
5	4	6	9	7	3	1	8	2

LOGIDOKU (page 73)

7	8	1	2	6	5	4	3	9
3	2	6	4	8	9	7	1	5
4	9	5	7	1	3	2	8	6
9	1	4	6	2	8	5	7	3
5	6	3	9	4	7	8	2	1
2	7	8	5	3	1	9	6	4
1	4	7	8	9	6	3	5	2
8	3	2	1	5	4	6	9	7
6	5	9	3	7	2	1	4	8

SUDOKU (page 71)

2	5	8	7	9	3	1	6	4
7	3	1	5	4	6	2	8	9
9	6	4	1	2	8	5	7	3
1	7	9	4	8	2	6	3	5
4	2	5	3	6	7	9	1	8
6	8	3	9	1	5	4	2	7
5	1	2	8	3	4	7	9	6
3	4	6	2	7	9	8	5	1
8	9	7	6	5	1	3	4	2

SUDOKU (page 74)

9	3	5	1	2	7	4	6	8
1	6	7	4	5	8	3	9	2
2	8	4	9	6	3	1	5	7
8	5	1	7	3	4	9	2	6
7	2	9	6	8	1	5	3	4
6	4	3	5	9	2	8	7	1
4	7	2	3	1	9	6	8	5
5	9	8	2	4	6	7	1	3
3	1	6	8	7	5	2	4	9

SUDOKU (page 72)

3	4	9	2	6	7	1	5	8
2	8	6	4	1	5	3	7	9
7	1	5	8	3	9	4	6	2
5	7	1	6	8	4	9	2	3
6	2	3	7	9	1	8	4	5
8	9	4	5	2	3	7	1	6
9	6	2	1	4	8	5	3	7
1	3	7	9	5	6	2	8	4
4	5	8	3	7	2	6	9	1

SUDOKU (page 75)

5	1	2	3	6	9	4	8	7
3	4	6	2	8	7	9	5	1
7	8	9	4	5	1	3	2	6
2	6	5	9	1	3	8	7	4
8	9	4	5	7	2	1	6	3
1	7	3	8	4	6	2	9	5
9	2	1	6	3	5	7	4	8
4	5	7	1	2	8	6	3	9
6	3	8	7	9	4	5	1	2

ANSWERS

SUDOKU (page 76)

7	1	6	2	3	5	9	8	4
2	3	8	9	6	4	1	7	5
9	5	4	7	8	1	3	2	6
6	9	2	8	5	7	4	1	3
8	4	3	1	9	2	5	6	7
1	7	5	6	4	3	8	9	2
4	6	7	5	1	9	2	3	8
3	8	9	4	2	6	7	5	1
5	2	1	3	7	8	6	4	9

SUDOKU (page 79)

6	7	2	5	4	3	8	1	9
5	1	8	2	6	9	4	3	7
4	3	9	8	1	7	2	5	6
3	2	4	9	8	6	5	7	1
8	9	5	4	7	1	3	6	2
7	6	1	3	2	5	9	4	8
1	5	3	6	9	8	7	2	4
9	4	7	1	3	2	6	8	5
2	8	6	7	5	4	1	9	3

SUDOKU (page 77)

3	6	1	7	8	4	9	2	5
2	9	4	5	6	3	7	8	1
8	5	7	2	1	9	3	4	6
4	8	6	1	9	5	2	3	7
9	1	2	3	7	8	5	6	4
5	7	3	4	2	6	1	9	8
1	3	8	9	4	7	6	5	2
7	4	9	6	5	2	8	1	3
6	2	5	8	3	1	4	7	9

CALCU-DOKU (page 80)

4	1	2	6	5	3
3	2	4	5	1	6
1	6	5	3	4	2
5	4	6	2	3	1
2	3	1	4	6	5
6	5	3	1	2	4

SUDOKU (page 78)

6	5	7	1	4	8	2	3	9
9	4	8	5	3	2	1	7	6
2	1	3	7	9	6	4	8	5
4	2	5	8	7	3	6	9	1
3	7	6	4	1	9	5	2	8
8	9	1	2	6	5	3	4	7
5	6	4	9	2	7	8	1	3
7	8	2	3	5	1	9	6	4
1	3	9	6	8	4	7	5	2

SUDOKU (page 81)

4	7	9	1	6	2	8	3	5
1	2	6	5	8	3	4	7	9
3	8	5	9	4	7	1	2	6
5	1	7	2	9	6	3	8	4
6	4	8	3	7	5	9	1	2
9	3	2	8	1	4	5	6	7
7	9	3	4	2	8	6	5	1
2	5	1	6	3	9	7	4	8
8	6	4	7	5	1	2	9	3

ANSWERS

SUDOKU (page 82)

8	4	2	1	6	5	9	3	7
3	5	7	2	9	4	1	6	8
1	9	6	3	8	7	4	2	5
2	6	3	5	7	1	8	4	9
7	1	9	6	4	8	2	5	3
4	8	5	9	2	3	6	7	1
9	3	4	8	5	2	7	1	6
5	2	8	7	1	6	3	9	4
6	7	1	4	3	9	5	8	2

SUDOKU (page 85)

6	2	7	3	4	1	5	9	8
5	8	1	2	9	6	4	3	7
3	4	9	7	8	5	2	1	6
7	5	2	8	1	3	9	6	4
1	6	4	9	5	2	8	7	3
9	3	8	4	6	7	1	5	2
8	7	3	1	2	9	6	4	5
2	9	5	6	7	4	3	8	1
4	1	6	5	3	8	7	2	9

SUDOKU (page 83)

3	7	9	2	8	6	5	4	1
8	5	4	3	1	7	9	2	6
2	6	1	5	9	4	8	3	7
6	3	5	4	2	1	7	9	8
4	1	7	8	6	9	3	5	2
9	8	2	7	3	5	6	1	4
5	4	6	9	7	2	1	8	3
1	2	3	6	5	8	4	7	9
7	9	8	1	4	3	2	6	5

ODD-EVEN LOGIDOKU (page 86)

3	7	5	9	1	2	6	4	8
9	4	1	8	5	6	7	3	2
2	6	8	3	7	4	9	5	1
1	3	7	6	9	5	8	2	4
4	5	9	1	2	8	3	7	6
6	8	2	4	3	7	5	1	9
5	2	6	7	4	9	1	8	3
8	1	4	5	6	3	2	9	7
7	9	3	2	8	1	4	6	5

SUDOKU (page 84)

8	5	6	4	2	7	1	3	9
3	7	1	5	6	9	8	4	2
9	2	4	8	1	3	7	6	5
7	4	3	2	9	8	6	5	1
1	9	8	6	5	4	3	2	7
2	6	5	3	7	1	4	9	8
4	3	9	1	8	2	5	7	6
5	8	7	9	3	6	2	1	4
6	1	2	7	4	5	9	8	3

SUDOKU (page 87)

2	4	6	5	7	8	9	3	1
8	9	7	4	1	3	5	6	2
3	5	1	9	2	6	8	4	7
7	2	9	3	8	4	6	1	5
6	1	4	2	5	7	3	8	9
5	8	3	1	6	9	2	7	4
9	6	5	8	4	1	7	2	3
1	3	8	7	9	2	4	5	6
4	7	2	6	3	5	1	9	8

ANSWERS

SUDOKU (page 88)

1	6	4	8	2	9	7	3	5
2	3	8	7	5	1	4	6	9
9	7	5	4	3	6	2	8	1
6	2	1	5	8	3	9	7	4
5	9	3	6	4	7	8	1	2
8	4	7	1	9	2	3	5	6
7	5	9	2	1	8	6	4	3
4	8	2	3	6	5	1	9	7
3	1	6	9	7	4	5	2	8

SUDOKU (page 91)

5	2	4	9	1	7	3	8	6
9	8	6	3	2	5	4	1	7
3	1	7	4	8	6	5	9	2
6	5	1	7	3	4	9	2	8
2	4	3	1	9	8	7	6	5
8	7	9	5	6	2	1	3	4
1	6	5	2	4	9	8	7	3
4	9	8	6	7	3	2	5	1
7	3	2	8	5	1	6	4	9

SUDOKU (page 89)

8	4	6	2	5	7	3	1	9
9	1	3	4	8	6	2	5	7
5	2	7	3	9	1	6	8	4
1	6	5	9	3	2	4	7	8
3	7	4	5	1	8	9	2	6
2	8	9	7	6	4	5	3	1
7	5	1	6	2	9	8	4	3
4	9	2	8	7	3	1	6	5
6	3	8	1	4	5	7	9	2

CALCU-DOKU (page 92)

3	4	1	2
1	3	2	4
2	1	4	3
4	2	3	1

SUDOKU (page 90)

3	8	4	6	5	1	9	2	7
5	6	2	7	9	4	1	8	3
1	7	9	8	3	2	6	5	4
9	5	6	1	4	3	2	7	8
7	4	1	5	2	8	3	6	9
2	3	8	9	7	6	5	4	1
6	2	3	4	8	9	7	1	5
4	9	5	2	1	7	8	3	6
8	1	7	3	6	5	4	9	2

SUDOKU (page 93)

5	3	1	7	9	2	4	6	8
6	4	2	8	3	5	1	9	7
7	9	8	1	4	6	2	5	3
2	5	4	9	7	1	3	8	6
8	1	7	2	6	3	5	4	9
3	6	9	4	5	8	7	2	1
9	2	3	5	8	7	6	1	4
4	7	5	6	1	9	8	3	2
1	8	6	3	2	4	9	7	5

ANSWERS

SUDOKU (page 94)

4	7	2	1	9	8	3	6	5
9	5	6	4	3	7	2	1	8
8	3	1	5	6	2	9	7	4
2	8	7	6	1	4	5	3	9
3	1	9	8	7	5	4	2	6
5	6	4	9	2	3	7	8	1
1	2	8	7	4	9	6	5	3
6	4	3	2	5	1	8	9	7
7	9	5	3	8	6	1	4	2

SUDOKU (page 97)

8	1	6	3	4	5	7	9	2
5	2	4	1	9	7	6	3	8
9	3	7	6	2	8	1	4	5
6	4	5	2	1	9	3	8	7
3	7	9	8	5	6	2	1	4
1	8	2	7	3	4	5	6	9
7	5	3	4	8	1	9	2	6
4	6	1	9	7	2	8	5	3
2	9	8	5	6	3	4	7	1

SUDOKU (page 95)

2	4	7	3	1	5	9	6	8
6	1	3	7	9	8	4	5	2
9	8	5	6	2	4	7	1	3
5	3	4	9	8	6	1	2	7
7	2	8	4	5	1	3	9	6
1	9	6	2	3	7	8	4	5
8	6	9	1	7	2	5	3	4
3	7	2	5	4	9	6	8	1
4	5	1	8	6	3	2	7	9

SUDOKU (page 98)

3	6	5	9	7	2	1	8	4
8	7	1	6	4	5	9	3	2
4	9	2	1	3	8	6	5	7
1	3	9	2	5	6	7	4	8
2	4	8	7	9	3	5	6	1
6	5	7	8	1	4	2	9	3
9	8	4	5	2	1	3	7	6
5	2	6	3	8	7	4	1	9
7	1	3	4	6	9	8	2	5

SUDOKU (page 96)

1	7	2	6	3	4	9	5	8
9	6	8	1	5	7	4	2	3
3	5	4	9	8	2	6	1	7
7	2	3	5	9	1	8	6	4
6	8	5	4	7	3	1	9	2
4	1	9	2	6	8	3	7	5
8	4	6	7	2	9	5	3	1
2	9	1	3	4	5	7	8	6
5	3	7	8	1	6	2	4	9

ODD-EVEN LOGIDOKU (page 99)

1	5	2	8	7	9	6	4	3
8	3	9	6	4	2	1	5	7
4	7	6	1	5	3	2	8	9
3	4	8	7	1	6	9	2	5
6	9	1	2	8	5	7	3	4
5	2	7	9	3	4	8	1	6
9	6	4	3	2	8	5	7	1
2	1	3	5	6	7	4	9	8
7	8	5	4	9	1	3	6	2

ANSWERS

SUDOKU (page 100)

7	5	9	4	8	3	1	6	2
2	3	4	9	6	1	5	8	7
6	8	1	5	2	7	4	9	3
8	2	6	3	5	4	7	1	9
9	1	3	6	7	2	8	4	5
4	7	5	1	9	8	2	3	6
1	4	7	2	3	9	6	5	8
5	9	2	8	4	6	3	7	1
3	6	8	7	1	5	9	2	4

SUDOKU (page 103)

6	1	8	2	7	3	5	4	9
2	9	3	5	8	4	6	1	7
4	7	5	9	1	6	8	3	2
7	2	4	1	6	8	9	5	3
3	5	6	4	9	2	7	8	1
1	8	9	7	3	5	2	6	4
5	4	1	8	2	7	3	9	6
9	3	2	6	5	1	4	7	8
8	6	7	3	4	9	1	2	5

SUDOKU (page 101)

7	3	1	8	9	2	6	4	5
5	6	2	4	3	7	1	9	8
4	8	9	5	1	6	2	7	3
1	7	6	3	2	4	5	8	9
2	4	8	9	5	1	3	6	7
3	9	5	7	6	8	4	2	1
6	5	4	1	8	9	7	3	2
9	2	3	6	7	5	8	1	4
8	1	7	2	4	3	9	5	6

SUDOKU (page 104)

7	5	6	8	2	9	1	3	4
9	4	1	6	3	7	5	8	2
3	2	8	5	4	1	7	9	6
2	6	3	1	9	8	4	5	7
1	8	7	4	6	5	3	2	9
4	9	5	2	7	3	6	1	8
5	1	9	7	8	4	2	6	3
6	3	4	9	1	2	8	7	5
8	7	2	3	5	6	9	4	1

SUDOKU (page 102)

2	5	6	1	7	8	3	9	4
4	8	9	2	3	6	5	1	7
7	3	1	9	4	5	8	6	2
8	1	3	7	9	4	6	2	5
5	4	2	3	6	1	7	8	9
9	6	7	8	5	2	1	4	3
6	2	5	4	8	7	9	3	1
1	9	8	5	2	3	4	7	6
3	7	4	6	1	9	2	5	8

CALCU-DOKU (page 105)

6	3	4	1	5	2
4	5	1	2	6	3
1	2	5	6	3	4
2	6	3	4	1	5
3	1	2	5	4	6
5	4	6	3	2	1

ANSWERS

SUDOKU (page 106)

5	9	1	8	2	3	4	6	7
6	2	4	7	1	9	5	3	8
3	8	7	5	4	6	1	2	9
9	1	3	2	5	4	7	8	6
7	6	5	9	8	1	2	4	3
2	4	8	6	3	7	9	5	1
8	5	9	1	6	2	3	7	4
4	7	2	3	9	8	6	1	5
1	3	6	4	7	5	8	9	2

SUDOKU (page 109)

6	3	5	4	8	7	1	2	9
1	9	8	5	2	6	3	4	7
4	7	2	1	9	3	5	6	8
9	6	1	3	7	4	2	8	5
5	2	3	8	1	9	4	7	6
7	8	4	6	5	2	9	1	3
2	4	9	7	6	5	8	3	1
8	5	7	2	3	1	6	9	4
3	1	6	9	4	8	7	5	2

SUDOKU (page 107)

2	3	4	1	6	9	7	5	8
5	9	8	3	7	4	6	2	1
1	6	7	5	8	2	3	4	9
8	1	6	2	5	7	9	3	4
7	2	9	4	3	1	5	8	6
3	4	5	8	9	6	2	1	7
9	5	3	7	4	8	1	6	2
4	7	1	6	2	5	8	9	3
6	8	2	9	1	3	4	7	5

SUDOKU (page 110)

4	1	5	8	2	6	7	3	9
9	6	7	1	4	3	2	5	8
3	8	2	7	5	9	4	1	6
2	4	9	6	3	8	5	7	1
7	5	8	4	1	2	9	6	3
1	3	6	9	7	5	8	2	4
5	9	1	3	8	7	6	4	2
8	7	4	2	6	1	3	9	5
6	2	3	5	9	4	1	8	7

SUDOKU (page 108)

6	8	9	5	4	7	3	1	2
7	4	2	6	1	3	5	9	8
3	1	5	8	9	2	7	4	6
9	2	6	1	5	4	8	7	3
8	3	4	2	7	6	1	5	9
1	5	7	3	8	9	6	2	4
2	7	1	4	3	8	9	6	5
4	9	8	7	6	5	2	3	1
5	6	3	9	2	1	4	8	7

SUDOKU (page 111)

7	3	8	2	1	9	6	4	5
1	5	4	3	7	6	8	2	9
6	9	2	4	8	5	1	3	7
5	8	6	1	4	3	9	7	2
2	1	3	9	5	7	4	8	6
4	7	9	6	2	8	3	5	1
8	6	7	5	9	4	2	1	3
3	2	5	8	6	1	7	9	4
9	4	1	7	3	2	5	6	8

ANSWERS

ODD-EVEN LOGIDOKU (page 112)

8	4	6	3	9	7	5	1	2
9	2	1	8	5	4	6	3	7
5	3	7	1	6	2	9	4	8
7	9	5	4	3	6	8	2	1
3	6	2	7	1	8	4	9	5
1	8	4	5	2	9	7	6	3
2	5	8	6	4	1	3	7	9
6	7	9	2	8	3	1	5	4
4	1	3	9	7	5	2	8	6

SUDOKU (page 115)

1	8	6	4	2	7	5	9	3
9	3	4	1	8	5	2	6	7
7	5	2	9	3	6	1	8	4
5	1	3	7	6	4	8	2	9
4	9	7	2	5	8	6	3	1
6	2	8	3	9	1	4	7	5
3	6	1	5	7	2	9	4	8
8	4	9	6	1	3	7	5	2
2	7	5	8	4	9	3	1	6

SUDOKU (page 113)

5	1	4	3	6	7	9	2	8
3	2	8	1	4	9	6	5	7
7	6	9	8	5	2	3	4	1
4	8	7	2	9	6	1	3	5
2	9	1	4	3	5	8	7	6
6	5	3	7	8	1	2	9	4
1	7	5	9	2	8	4	6	3
8	4	2	6	7	3	5	1	9
9	3	6	5	1	4	7	8	2

SUDOKU (page 116)

5	9	8	4	7	1	6	2	3
6	2	3	8	9	5	1	4	7
7	1	4	6	2	3	5	9	8
1	5	9	7	6	4	3	8	2
3	8	6	9	5	2	7	1	4
2	4	7	3	1	8	9	5	6
8	6	1	5	4	7	2	3	9
9	3	2	1	8	6	4	7	5
4	7	5	2	3	9	8	6	1

SUDOKU (page 114)

2	1	7	4	9	8	3	5	6
9	3	4	7	6	5	8	2	1
8	5	6	2	3	1	7	9	4
1	6	9	3	2	4	5	7	8
5	4	3	8	1	7	2	6	9
7	2	8	6	5	9	1	4	3
3	7	1	5	4	6	9	8	2
4	8	2	9	7	3	6	1	5
6	9	5	1	8	2	4	3	7

SUDOKU (page 117)

6	9	5	2	8	7	3	1	4
2	4	7	3	1	9	8	6	5
8	3	1	5	4	6	9	7	2
4	1	2	7	5	3	6	9	8
7	5	6	4	9	8	2	3	1
3	8	9	6	2	1	5	4	7
1	6	3	8	7	2	4	5	9
5	7	8	9	3	4	1	2	6
9	2	4	1	6	5	7	8	3

ANSWERS

CALCU-DOKU (page 118)

2	3	6	5	1	4
6	4	5	2	3	1
5	1	4	3	6	2
3	5	1	4	2	6
1	2	3	6	4	5
4	6	2	1	5	3

SUDOKU (page 121)

3	8	9	5	4	2	1	6	7
7	1	5	6	9	8	4	2	3
2	4	6	1	7	3	9	8	5
4	6	8	7	2	9	5	3	1
9	7	1	3	6	5	2	4	8
5	2	3	8	1	4	6	7	9
8	9	2	4	3	1	7	5	6
1	5	7	2	8	6	3	9	4
6	3	4	9	5	7	8	1	2

SUDOKU (page 119)

4	5	3	8	9	2	7	6	1
1	7	8	6	3	4	2	9	5
6	2	9	5	1	7	8	3	4
5	1	6	2	8	9	4	7	3
3	9	7	1	4	6	5	2	8
8	4	2	7	5	3	6	1	9
2	8	4	3	7	1	9	5	6
7	3	5	9	6	8	1	4	2
9	6	1	4	2	5	3	8	7

SUDOKU (page 122)

6	1	4	5	3	8	9	7	2
2	8	3	1	7	9	4	6	5
7	5	9	6	4	2	1	3	8
8	2	6	4	9	1	7	5	3
3	4	1	7	8	5	6	2	9
5	9	7	2	6	3	8	4	1
9	6	8	3	2	7	5	1	4
1	7	2	8	5	4	3	9	6
4	3	5	9	1	6	2	8	7

SUDOKU (page 120)

2	4	9	5	1	6	8	3	7
1	6	7	8	3	9	4	2	5
8	3	5	7	2	4	6	9	1
6	7	3	9	4	1	5	8	2
9	2	1	6	5	8	7	4	3
5	8	4	3	7	2	9	1	6
3	1	6	4	9	5	2	7	8
7	9	8	2	6	3	1	5	4
4	5	2	1	8	7	3	6	9

SUDOKU (page 123)

9	4	7	1	2	3	6	8	5
3	2	8	5	4	6	9	7	1
5	6	1	8	9	7	3	4	2
7	9	4	2	8	5	1	6	3
2	8	6	7	3	1	4	5	9
1	5	3	4	6	9	8	2	7
6	1	2	3	5	4	7	9	8
4	3	5	9	7	8	2	1	6
8	7	9	6	1	2	5	3	4

ANSWERS

SUDOKU (page 124)

8	7	2	6	4	5	1	3	9
9	3	4	1	2	8	6	5	7
5	1	6	3	9	7	8	4	2
4	6	5	2	1	9	3	7	8
2	9	7	8	6	3	4	1	5
1	8	3	5	7	4	9	2	6
6	4	1	7	8	2	5	9	3
7	5	9	4	3	6	2	8	1
3	2	8	9	5	1	7	6	4

SUDOKU (page 127)

3	8	5	7	9	6	1	4	2
2	6	4	5	1	8	3	7	9
9	1	7	3	2	4	6	5	8
5	4	1	9	8	2	7	6	3
8	7	9	6	3	5	4	2	1
6	3	2	4	7	1	8	9	5
4	2	3	8	5	7	9	1	6
1	9	6	2	4	3	5	8	7
7	5	8	1	6	9	2	3	4

ODD-EVEN LOGIDOKU (page 125)

7	5	1	6	3	2	9	4	8
4	6	2	9	8	5	1	7	3
3	9	8	7	1	4	6	5	2
8	4	7	2	9	3	5	6	1
9	1	5	8	4	6	2	3	7
2	3	6	5	7	1	4	8	9
5	7	9	4	2	8	3	1	6
6	2	3	1	5	7	8	9	4
1	8	4	3	6	9	7	2	5

SUDOKU (page 128)

3	6	2	1	8	9	5	4	7
1	7	8	3	4	5	6	9	2
9	4	5	2	6	7	3	1	8
6	2	3	7	1	4	8	5	9
5	1	7	8	9	6	2	3	4
8	9	4	5	3	2	7	6	1
2	3	1	4	5	8	9	7	6
7	5	9	6	2	1	4	8	3
4	8	6	9	7	3	1	2	5

SUDOKU (page 126)

1	4	8	2	3	7	5	9	6
5	6	9	8	4	1	2	3	7
3	2	7	6	5	9	4	1	8
8	3	4	1	7	6	9	5	2
6	1	5	9	2	4	8	7	3
9	7	2	5	8	3	6	4	1
2	9	3	7	6	5	1	8	4
4	8	1	3	9	2	7	6	5
7	5	6	4	1	8	3	2	9

SUDOKU (page 129)

3	5	6	1	7	8	9	4	2
1	7	9	2	3	4	8	6	5
4	8	2	6	9	5	1	7	3
9	4	1	5	8	7	2	3	6
8	2	7	4	6	3	5	9	1
5	6	3	9	1	2	4	8	7
7	3	4	8	2	1	6	5	9
2	9	8	3	5	6	7	1	4
6	1	5	7	4	9	3	2	8

ANSWERS

SUDOKU (page 130)

8	5	3	4	7	6	1	2	9
1	4	9	3	5	2	6	8	7
2	6	7	1	9	8	3	5	4
3	1	8	5	6	4	9	7	2
7	2	4	9	8	3	5	6	1
5	9	6	7	2	1	8	4	3
4	8	2	6	1	9	7	3	5
9	3	5	8	4	7	2	1	6
6	7	1	2	3	5	4	9	8

CALCU-DOKU (page 131)

1	5	2	4	3	6
5	3	4	6	1	2
6	4	5	1	2	3
3	1	6	2	4	5
2	6	1	3	5	4
4	2	3	5	6	1

SUDOKU (page 132)

8	2	7	4	6	9	1	5	3
6	1	5	2	8	3	7	4	9
4	9	3	5	1	7	8	6	2
2	6	4	7	5	8	3	9	1
7	3	9	1	2	6	4	8	5
5	8	1	3	9	4	2	7	6
9	4	2	6	7	1	5	3	8
3	5	8	9	4	2	6	1	7
1	7	6	8	3	5	9	2	4

SUDOKU (page 133)

6	3	9	2	1	7	4	8	5
4	8	2	5	9	6	1	3	7
1	5	7	4	3	8	6	2	9
3	9	5	8	2	1	7	6	4
2	4	1	6	7	3	9	5	8
7	6	8	9	5	4	3	1	2
8	2	4	3	6	9	5	7	1
5	7	6	1	4	2	8	9	3
9	1	3	7	8	5	2	4	6

SUDOKU (page 134)

7	9	3	4	5	8	1	2	6
2	5	1	6	7	3	9	8	4
8	6	4	9	2	1	5	3	7
1	3	2	5	6	4	7	9	8
5	4	8	7	3	9	2	6	1
9	7	6	8	1	2	4	5	3
3	1	5	2	4	6	8	7	9
4	2	9	3	8	7	6	1	5
6	8	7	1	9	5	3	4	2

SUDOKU (page 135)

9	8	6	5	7	2	4	3	1
4	5	7	3	8	1	2	9	6
2	1	3	9	4	6	5	8	7
5	6	9	2	3	8	1	7	4
8	7	1	4	6	5	3	2	9
3	4	2	1	9	7	8	6	5
6	9	5	8	2	4	7	1	3
1	3	8	7	5	9	6	4	2
7	2	4	6	1	3	9	5	8

ANSWERS

SUDOKU (page 136)

1	7	4	2	9	5	8	3	6
3	5	2	6	7	8	9	4	1
6	9	8	3	1	4	2	5	7
5	8	9	4	6	1	7	2	3
7	4	3	8	5	2	1	6	9
2	1	6	9	3	7	4	8	5
9	2	7	5	4	3	6	1	8
4	6	5	1	8	9	3	7	2
8	3	1	7	2	6	5	9	4

SUDOKU (page 139)

3	9	7	4	1	8	6	5	2
5	4	6	2	3	9	8	1	7
8	2	1	6	5	7	9	4	3
7	1	3	8	4	2	5	9	6
4	6	5	9	7	1	2	3	8
9	8	2	3	6	5	1	7	4
2	5	4	1	8	3	7	6	9
6	7	8	5	9	4	3	2	1
1	3	9	7	2	6	4	8	5

SUDOKU (page 137)

2	3	1	6	9	8	5	4	7
9	6	5	2	7	4	8	1	3
8	4	7	1	5	3	9	6	2
7	2	6	3	1	9	4	5	8
1	5	3	4	8	6	7	2	9
4	9	8	7	2	5	1	3	6
6	1	9	5	3	7	2	8	4
3	8	2	9	4	1	6	7	5
5	7	4	8	6	2	3	9	1

SUDOKU (page 140)

4	6	7	1	3	5	9	2	8
1	2	9	4	8	6	5	7	3
8	5	3	2	7	9	6	4	1
5	1	4	7	6	2	8	3	9
6	9	2	8	1	3	7	5	4
3	7	8	9	5	4	1	6	2
2	8	1	6	4	7	3	9	5
7	4	5	3	9	1	2	8	6
9	3	6	5	2	8	4	1	7

ODD-EVEN LOGIDOKU (page 138)

8	6	5	7	3	2	1	9	4
7	4	3	9	1	6	2	5	8
1	2	9	8	5	4	3	7	6
3	9	8	1	4	7	5	6	2
2	7	4	5	6	9	8	1	3
5	1	6	2	8	3	9	4	7
6	5	1	4	2	8	7	3	9
4	8	7	3	9	5	6	2	1
9	3	2	6	7	1	4	8	5

SUDOKU (page 141)

6	5	1	9	7	3	4	8	2
2	4	7	5	8	1	3	6	9
9	3	8	2	6	4	1	5	7
3	7	2	6	5	9	8	1	4
1	8	9	4	3	7	5	2	6
5	6	4	1	2	8	9	7	3
7	1	3	8	9	6	2	4	5
8	2	6	3	4	5	7	9	1
4	9	5	7	1	2	6	3	8

ANSWERS

SUDOKU (page 142)

2	1	9	6	8	4	5	3	7
5	4	3	9	7	2	8	6	1
8	7	6	5	1	3	2	9	4
6	3	7	4	2	5	9	1	8
1	9	2	8	6	7	4	5	3
4	8	5	3	9	1	6	7	2
7	2	8	1	5	6	3	4	9
9	6	4	7	3	8	1	2	5
3	5	1	2	4	9	7	8	6

SUDOKU (page 145)

2	9	1	7	8	5	6	4	3
4	6	7	2	9	3	5	8	1
3	5	8	4	6	1	9	7	2
8	7	9	5	1	2	4	3	6
6	3	5	9	4	7	2	1	8
1	2	4	8	3	6	7	9	5
9	4	6	1	2	8	3	5	7
7	8	3	6	5	9	1	2	4
5	1	2	3	7	4	8	6	9

SUDOKU (page 143)

3	4	9	1	7	2	5	6	8
6	7	1	8	3	5	2	4	9
2	8	5	9	6	4	7	3	1
8	1	3	2	5	7	4	9	6
5	6	7	4	9	1	8	2	3
9	2	4	3	8	6	1	5	7
7	9	8	5	2	3	6	1	4
1	5	6	7	4	9	3	8	2
4	3	2	6	1	8	9	7	5

SUDOKU (page 146)

8	3	9	6	4	2	5	1	7
2	4	7	1	5	8	6	9	3
6	1	5	3	7	9	8	4	2
4	7	1	9	3	6	2	8	5
5	6	2	8	1	4	3	7	9
3	9	8	7	2	5	4	6	1
9	5	4	2	6	7	1	3	8
7	2	3	4	8	1	9	5	6
1	8	6	5	9	3	7	2	4

CALCU-DOKU (page 144)

4	1	5	2	3
1	3	4	5	2
3	4	2	1	5
2	5	1	3	4
5	2	3	4	1

SUDOKU (page 147)

4	9	1	7	5	6	3	8	2
7	6	8	3	1	2	9	4	5
3	5	2	8	4	9	6	1	7
2	8	5	1	9	7	4	3	6
1	4	7	6	3	5	2	9	8
9	3	6	4	2	8	5	7	1
6	7	4	2	8	3	1	5	9
5	2	3	9	7	1	8	6	4
8	1	9	5	6	4	7	2	3

ANSWERS

SUDOKU (page 148)

9	1	8	2	4	5	7	6	3
3	2	7	6	8	1	4	5	9
4	6	5	7	9	3	1	8	2
2	7	1	9	5	6	8	3	4
5	4	6	3	7	8	9	2	1
8	9	3	1	2	4	5	7	6
7	8	2	4	6	9	3	1	5
1	5	9	8	3	2	6	4	7
6	3	4	5	1	7	2	9	8

ODD-EVEN LOGIDOKU (page 151)

7	9	4	3	6	1	2	8	5
6	8	1	2	9	5	7	3	4
3	2	5	4	8	7	9	1	6
1	5	2	6	3	8	4	9	7
8	6	9	7	4	2	3	5	1
4	3	7	1	5	9	8	6	2
9	4	6	5	2	3	1	7	8
5	7	3	8	1	4	6	2	9
2	1	8	9	7	6	5	4	3

SUDOKU (page 149)

8	1	2	3	9	5	6	7	4
4	9	6	1	8	7	5	2	3
3	5	7	4	2	6	8	9	1
6	8	9	2	5	1	4	3	7
5	2	4	7	6	3	1	8	9
1	7	3	9	4	8	2	6	5
9	6	5	8	7	4	3	1	2
7	3	8	5	1	2	9	4	6
2	4	1	6	3	9	7	5	8

SUDOKU (page 152)

2	9	8	6	1	7	5	3	4
3	1	7	4	5	9	6	8	2
5	4	6	8	3	2	1	9	7
1	3	5	2	9	4	7	6	8
6	8	9	5	7	3	2	4	1
7	2	4	1	6	8	9	5	3
8	7	2	9	4	5	3	1	6
9	6	3	7	8	1	4	2	5
4	5	1	3	2	6	8	7	9

SUDOKU (page 150)

5	2	1	6	8	3	4	7	9
8	4	3	7	1	9	6	5	2
7	9	6	2	5	4	3	8	1
6	3	5	1	9	7	2	4	8
2	8	9	5	4	6	1	3	7
1	7	4	3	2	8	5	9	6
4	5	8	9	6	2	7	1	3
9	6	7	4	3	1	8	2	5
3	1	2	8	7	5	9	6	4

SUDOKU (page 153)

8	5	4	6	7	3	1	2	9
9	7	3	8	2	1	4	6	5
2	1	6	9	4	5	8	3	7
4	2	7	1	5	8	3	9	6
6	8	1	3	9	7	5	4	2
5	3	9	4	6	2	7	8	1
3	6	5	7	8	9	2	1	4
7	9	8	2	1	4	6	5	3
1	4	2	5	3	6	9	7	8

ANSWERS

SUDOKU (page 154)

9	4	5	3	2	8	1	6	7
6	7	2	9	1	4	3	8	5
3	8	1	6	5	7	9	2	4
5	2	3	8	6	9	7	4	1
1	6	7	4	3	2	5	9	8
8	9	4	1	7	5	2	3	6
4	3	6	5	9	1	8	7	2
7	1	9	2	8	6	4	5	3
2	5	8	7	4	3	6	1	9

CALCU-DOKU (page 157)

5	6	3	1	2	4
6	2	5	4	3	1
3	5	1	6	4	2
1	4	2	3	5	6
4	3	6	2	1	5
2	1	4	5	6	3

SUDOKU (page 155)

9	1	8	6	7	3	5	2	4
6	7	5	9	4	2	3	8	1
2	4	3	5	8	1	7	6	9
5	2	6	8	3	4	1	9	7
1	3	9	2	6	7	8	4	5
7	8	4	1	5	9	2	3	6
3	6	2	4	1	5	9	7	8
4	5	7	3	9	8	6	1	2
8	9	1	7	2	6	4	5	3

SUDOKU (page 158)

7	4	5	8	3	9	2	1	6
9	3	2	6	7	1	5	4	8
6	8	1	2	4	5	3	9	7
5	6	3	7	9	4	8	2	1
8	7	4	1	5	2	9	6	3
1	2	9	3	8	6	4	7	5
2	9	8	5	1	7	6	3	4
3	1	6	4	2	8	7	5	9
4	5	7	9	6	3	1	8	2

SUDOKU (page 156)

2	7	9	5	4	1	6	3	8
3	1	6	8	2	9	7	4	5
8	5	4	6	3	7	1	9	2
6	9	5	3	8	2	4	1	7
1	8	3	4	7	5	2	6	9
4	2	7	9	1	6	5	8	3
9	3	1	7	5	4	8	2	6
7	4	8	2	6	3	9	5	1
5	6	2	1	9	8	3	7	4

SUDOKU (page 159)

2	3	7	1	5	9	8	4	6
9	1	6	3	8	4	7	5	2
5	8	4	7	6	2	3	9	1
3	6	2	5	4	1	9	8	7
4	5	1	9	7	8	2	6	3
8	7	9	2	3	6	4	1	5
6	2	8	4	1	7	5	3	9
7	4	5	6	9	3	1	2	8
1	9	3	8	2	5	6	7	4

ANSWERS

SUDOKU (page 160)

5	6	7	3	2	1	8	4	9
1	9	2	8	4	6	5	3	7
3	8	4	5	7	9	2	1	6
8	1	3	6	5	4	9	7	2
9	7	5	2	1	3	4	6	8
2	4	6	9	8	7	1	5	3
7	5	9	1	6	2	3	8	4
4	2	1	7	3	8	6	9	5
6	3	8	4	9	5	7	2	1

SUDOKU (page 163)

2	5	4	8	9	6	1	7	3
8	1	6	5	3	7	2	9	4
9	3	7	1	4	2	6	8	5
1	2	9	7	8	3	5	4	6
3	6	8	2	5	4	9	1	7
4	7	5	6	1	9	3	2	8
5	9	3	4	7	1	8	6	2
7	8	2	9	6	5	4	3	1
6	4	1	3	2	8	7	5	9

SUDOKU (page 161)

4	5	7	8	9	3	1	2	6
2	1	3	4	7	6	8	9	5
9	8	6	1	2	5	4	3	7
7	6	9	3	1	2	5	8	4
5	2	8	7	4	9	6	1	3
3	4	1	5	6	8	2	7	9
6	3	4	2	8	7	9	5	1
8	9	5	6	3	1	7	4	2
1	7	2	9	5	4	3	6	8

ODD-EVEN LOGIDOKU (page 164)

1	4	5	9	8	7	3	2	6
3	9	2	6	5	1	4	7	8
7	6	8	2	4	3	5	1	9
8	3	1	4	9	2	7	6	5
9	7	6	1	3	5	8	4	2
2	5	4	8	7	6	1	9	3
5	8	9	7	6	4	2	3	1
6	1	7	3	2	8	9	5	4
4	2	3	5	1	9	6	8	7

SUDOKU (page 162)

6	8	3	5	2	1	4	9	7
5	2	7	9	3	4	1	8	6
9	1	4	7	6	8	3	5	2
1	3	6	4	9	7	5	2	8
2	5	9	1	8	3	7	6	4
7	4	8	6	5	2	9	3	1
8	6	1	3	7	9	2	4	5
4	9	2	8	1	5	6	7	3
3	7	5	2	4	6	8	1	9

SUDOKU (page 165)

8	2	3	7	9	6	4	5	1
6	9	5	4	2	1	3	7	8
7	1	4	3	5	8	9	2	6
3	5	2	8	6	4	7	1	9
1	8	6	9	7	5	2	4	3
9	4	7	1	3	2	8	6	5
2	3	9	5	1	7	6	8	4
4	6	1	2	8	9	5	3	7
5	7	8	6	4	3	1	9	2